STABLEMATES

All Systems Go!

A Guide to the Horse's Fitness

The Pony Club
Stoneleigh Park
Kenilworth
Warwickshire
CV8 2RW

Website: www.pcuk.org

Stablemates Book 4: All Systems Go!
is published by The Pony Club

British Library Cataloguing in Publication Data.
A catalogue record for this book is available from the British Library.

ISBN 978-1-907279-12-6

Design and Production: Paul G. Harding

Printed by Halstan Printing Group in Amersham, UK
www.halstan.co.uk

Trade distribution by Kenilworth Press
An imprint of Quiller Publishing Ltd.
Wykey House, Wykey, Shrewsbury, SY4 1JA
Tel: 01939 261616 Fax: 01939 261606
E-mail: info@quillerbooks.com
Website: www.kenilworthpress.co.uk

STABLEMATES

All Systems Go!

A Guide to the Horse's Fitness

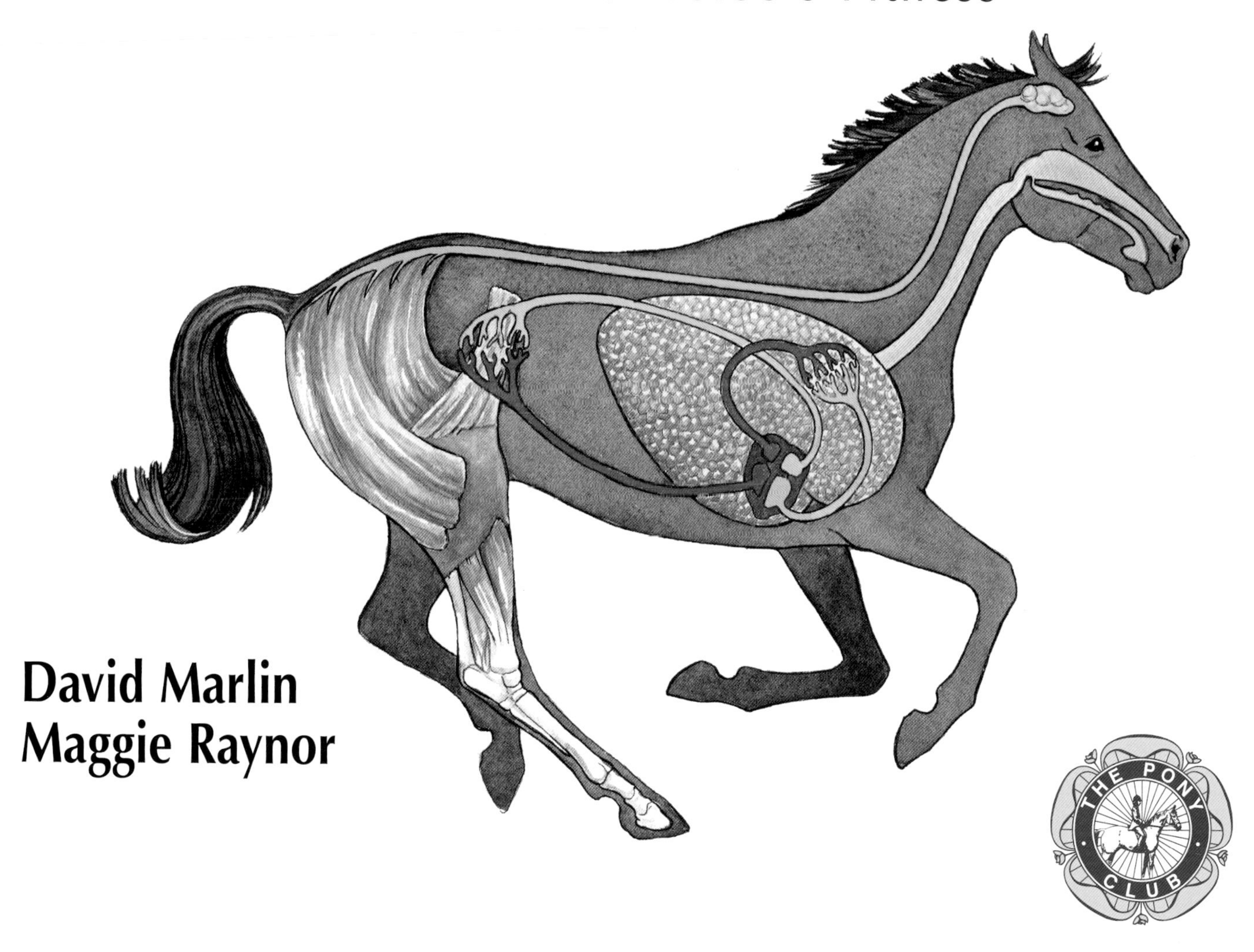

David Marlin
Maggie Raynor

Contents

Introduction

The horse is a truly amazing animal. It has the ability to run fast over short distances, as well as at a respectable pace over a hundred miles or more. It is able to jump over different heights and spreads of fences, and can learn and perform complex movements which involve considerable coordination and concentration. Even more amazingly, it manages to do all this with the weight of a rider on its back—weight which is far from insignificant! Imagine taking part in an athletics competition carrying a rucksack full of heavy books and you will begin to understand just what horses and ponies have to deal with when they are ridden.

Equally incredible is that within hours of being born a foal is able to get to its feet and canter with its mother: this, of course, being necessary for it to be able to survive in the wild. It has no way of defending itself, so if it were slow-moving it would be very vulnerable to predators and its mother would stand less chance of fighting them off. This is why foals are referred to as being *precocious*.

In the wild, horses spend most of their time eating, so they cover great distances at walk. Of course sometimes they may 'play', which can involve short periods of trot and canter. One of the few occasions when wild horses really canter fast, or gallop, is if they are surprised or threatened by predators. When this happens they usually gallop fast for a short distance, and once they feel safe they go back to eating. Another instance of noticeable activity is when stallions are fighting each other or showing off to mares. In the wild, therefore, the horse is really a sprinter—running very fast over a short distance and perhaps for only 20 to 30 seconds. These natural instincts and behaviours manifest themselves in showjumping (which is over short distances); quarter-horse racing (which consists of a quarter-of-a-mile gallop within a time of 20 seconds); polo (which involves repeated fast bouts of galloping interspersed with rest or recovery periods); and mounted games (which make the most of horses' and ponies' talents for rapid acceleration, precise turning and high speed over short distances). In contrast are the other skills required of horses and ponies in equestrian disciplines such as dressage, eventing, racing and endurance.

Understanding How a Horse's Body Works and the Importance of Fitness and Training

A horse is not a machine like a motorbike, car or even a bicycle, but he *does* have to be maintained and refuelled. You can put your car away in the garage for a few months and then get it out and expect it to be in the same condition and to perform in the same way as it did before. The major difference with a horse is that to get him suitably fit for what you will be expecting him to do you will need to train him.

If you ask too much of a horse you can expect two consequences: firstly, his performance may be very disappointing—in the same way as you would fail a spelling test if you didn't prepare for it adequately. Secondly, if you push him beyond his level of fitness he is likely to incur an injury.

Riding an unfit horse at medium speeds over long distances may lead to medical problems such as colic or muscle damage. Riding at higher speeds, over long distances, and jumping, may all increase the risk of a bone, joint, tendon or muscle injury, so it is necessary to understand that you need to train horses both to improve their performance and to help reduce the likelihood of injury or illness—which occur not only in competition but also frequently during training. In fact, in spite of all the efforts made to avoid injury, it is not uncommon for incorrect training to be the actual cause of it.

With a simple understanding of how your horse's body works and how it responds to exercise and training, it is possible to reduce the risk of injury by getting him in the right shape.

What is a Horse?

Like all living animals, horses are composed of single structures in the form of cells, of which there are many different types, such as muscle cells, liver cells, bone cells, nerve cells, kidney cells and skin cells. They are grouped together to form organs and structures such as the heart, lungs, kidneys and liver.

The various organs and structures of the horse may work together serving a common function, such as:

- *Circulatory system:* the heart, blood vessels and blood;
- *Respiratory system:* the lungs and airways that connect lungs to the outside (windpipe, throat, upper airways and nostrils);
- *Musculoskeletal system:* the muscles, bones, joints, tendons and ligaments;
- *Nervous system:* the brain, spinal cord (which runs within the bones that make up the spine or backbone) and all the nerves that come from the spinal cord;
- *Gastrointestinal system:* the mouth, oesophagus (the tube leading to the stomach), stomach and intestines;
- *Urinary system:* the kidneys, ureters (tubes connecting the kidneys to the bladder), bladder, and urethra (the tube that allows urine to leave the body);
- *Reproductive system:* the various genital structures and organs
- *Immune system:* a complex system of cells and proteins that protects the horse from elements foreign to the body, including allergens (moulds, pollens) and causes of infection (bacteria, virus, parasites, etc.);
- *Endocrine system:* along with the nervous system, this controls what happens within the body via chemical messages (known as *hormones*—such as adrenaline) that pass around the body in the bloodstream;
- *Integumentary system:* the skin and the hair (coat).

Of course, not all systems are important at all times or in all situations. For example, the reproductive system does not perform any important function during exercise.

The Respiratory System

The respiratory system consists of the lungs and associated airways (both inside the lungs and connecting the lungs to the outside environment). The functions of the respiratory system are:

- To provide the body with oxygen via the blood;
- To remove carbon dioxide from the blood;
- To help cool the horse down (blowing or panting);
- To enable the horse to use his sense of smell;
- To enable the horse to communicate by neighing, squealing, or snorting.

Air enters the respiratory tract through the nostrils only because, unlike in humans, the horse cannot breathe through his mouth. The air passes through the nostrils and is warmed and humidified in the nasal turbinates and nasopharynx before continuing through the larynx and into the trachea (or windpipe). The trachea is an oval-shaped tube, roughly 80cm long in a 500kg horse, and has around 50 to 60 rings of cartilage which prevent it from collapsing inwards when the horse breathes in during exercise. As the trachea enters the chest it tilts upwards and close to where it enters the lungs it divides into two bronchi: one of these goes into the left lung, and the other into the right. Further down inside the lungs the bronchi

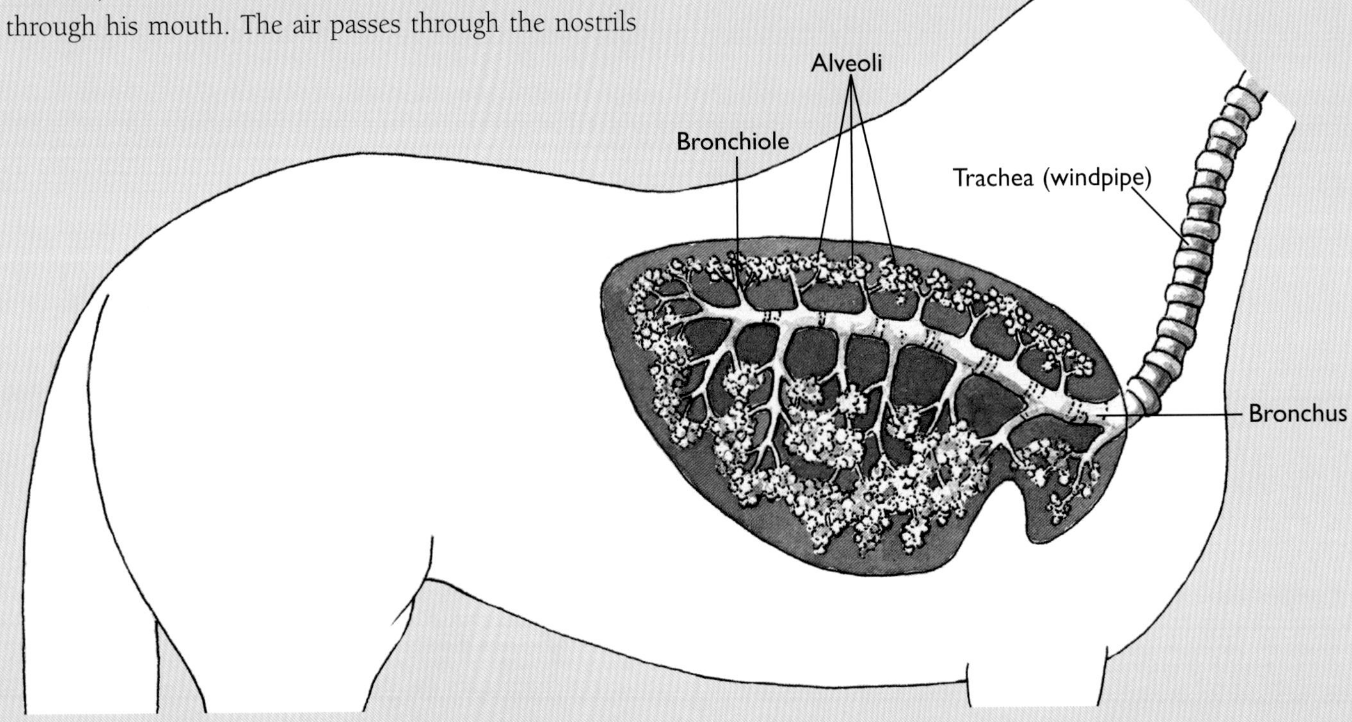

POSITION AND STRUCTURE OF THE LUNGS

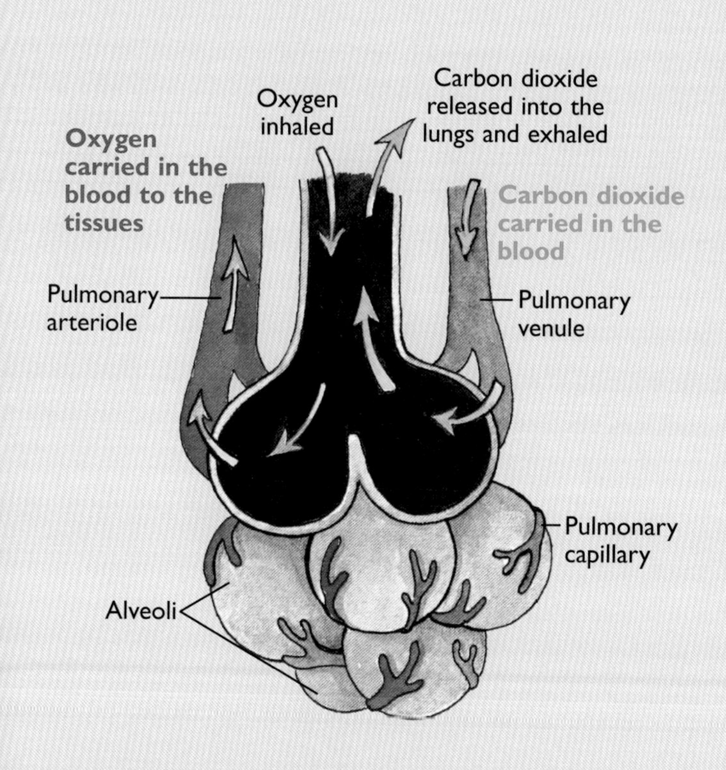

ALVEOLI SHOWING THE PROCESS OF GASEOUS EXCHANGE

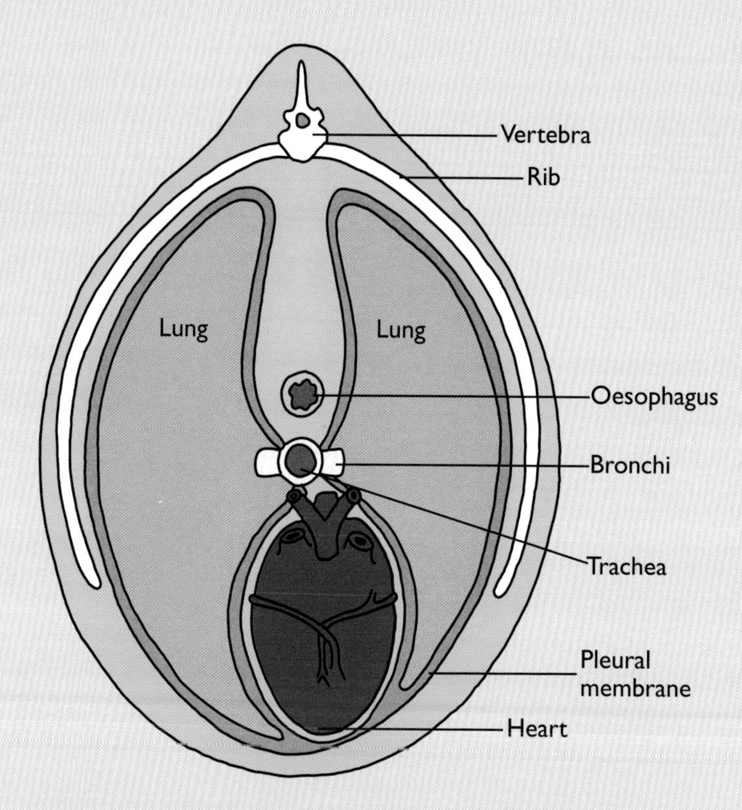

CROSS-SECTION THROUGH THE THORAX TO SHOW THE POSITION OF THE HEART AND LUNGS (VIEWED FROM THE FRONT OF THE HORSE)

divide into smaller airways known as *bronchioles* which, in turn, also subdivide into *alveolar ducts*. The alveolar ducts consist of millions of air sacs (*alveoli*) inside which the exchange of gases between the blood and the lungs takes place. The walls of the alveoli are very thin, and this allows the inhaled oxygen to pass through into the capillaries and carbon dioxide to pass back from the blood into the airspaces. The reason this gaseous exchange takes place is due to differences in the concentration of the gases in the air breathed in and in the blood: there is a high level of oxygen in air breathed in, but a low level in the blood, and as a result the oxygen moves from the area of high concentration to the area of low concentration by the process of diffusion. Similarly, carbon dioxide levels are high in the blood entering the lungs but low in the airspaces, so it moves in the opposite way to oxygen. Once inside the capillaries, almost all the oxygen binds itself to haemoglobin inside red blood cells, and this is how it is transported around the body. (Only a very small amount of dissolved oxygen is transported in the blood plasma.)

The Circulatory System

The circulatory system consists of the heart, the network of blood vessels, and the blood. The heart pumps blood through the arteries to the capillaries (which infiltrate almost all tissues and organs within the body). The blood returns back to the heart through the capillaries and veins. In this way, blood reaches almost every living cell in the body. The functions of the circulatory system are:

- To transport oxygen, water and nutrients around the body to the cells;
- To remove waste products from the body;
- To protect the body from infection by circulating white blood cells;
- To control body temperature;
- To move hormones from sites where they are produced—such as the brain—to the places where they act—such as the kidneys.

The heart is situated to the left of the horse's chest and is made up of a special kind of muscle (*cardiac muscle*) which contracts and relaxes continuously. Within the heart, a small collection of cells, known as the *pacemaker*, generates the beat, but the rate of pumping can be affected by a number of different factors, including nerves, circulating hormones, and the amount of blood flowing into the heart. The pumping of the heart cannot be controlled by the horse and is a totally automatic function (just the same as other automatic functions such as digestion). The interior of the heart is divided into four chambers: those at the top are smaller and known as the *right atrium* and *left atrium* (and together as the *atria*) and collect blood and 'store' it until they contract and push the blood down into the two lower chambers—the *ventricles*. The ventricles are the parts of the heart that produce the pressure to force the blood either to the lungs (from the right ventricle) or around the body in the arteries (from the left ventricle). The left ventricle is more muscular than the right and this

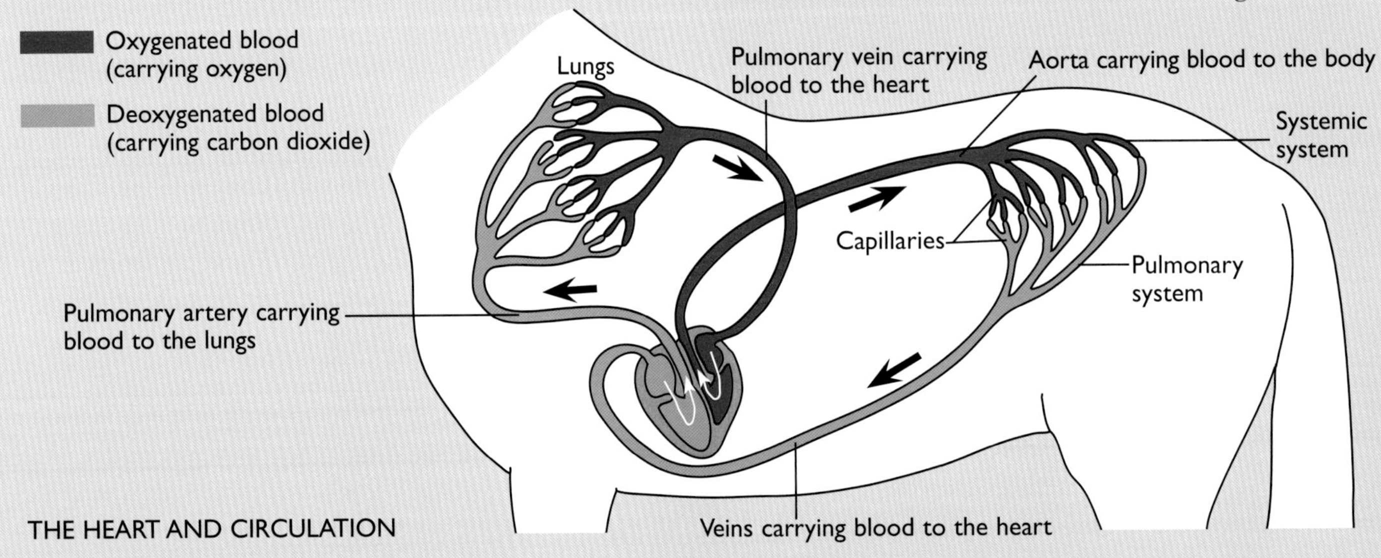

THE HEART AND CIRCULATION

relates to the fact that the blood in the left-hand side of the heart and arterial circulation is under much higher pressure.

Two distinct sounds can be heard in every heartbeat. The first is made by the closing of the tricuspid and mitral (or *bicuspid*) valves. The tricuspid valve is between the right atrium and the right ventricle, and the mitral valve is between the left atrium and the left ventricle. The second sound is made by the closing of the aortic and pulmonary valves. The aortic valve is between the left ventricle and the aorta (the main artery taking blood out of the heart under high pressure) and the pulmonary valves are between the right ventricle and the pulmonary artery which takes blood to the lungs.

Blood is carried away from the heart in arteries and towards the heart in veins. Generally-speaking, arteries carry oxygenated blood, and veins carry deoxygenated blood. When blood passes through tissue, the tissue removes a large amount of the oxygen carried in it; the only exceptions being the pulmonary artery (which carries deoxygenated (or *venous*) blood from the right ventricle to the lungs) and the pulmonary veins (which bring back oxygenated (or *arterial*) blood from the lungs to the heart). The part of the circulation that carries blood to and from the lungs is known as the *pulmonary circulation*, and the part of the circulation that carries blood around the rest of the body is known as the *systemic circulation*. One other special circulation is the *coronary circulation*—which supplies the heart itself.

Arteries have thicker walls than veins to withstand the higher pressures as blood is pumped through them by the heart and to help maintain the blood pressure. An artery can change diameter (due to contraction or relaxation of the muscles in its walls) to increase or decrease the flow of blood to any particular part of the body. If the horse is galloping, for example, the aorta (which is the main artery from the heart) will widen to accommodate the increased amount of blood being pumped out of the left ventricle at higher pressure, and this allows more blood to reach the muscles. Blood is pushed around the body and to the tissues because of the high pressure in the arteries, but as the blood passes through the capillary beds in the tissues the pressure, and hence the flow, drops considerably. The blood pressure in the venous circulation is about ten to twenty times less than in the major arteries. The contraction of muscles helps to squeeze the blood through the veins and one-way valves in the veins ensure that blood always flows towards the heart.

The arteries carry oxygen, hormones, nutrients and fluids to the cells that make up tissues and organs. The veins carry waste products and heat from the cells to the appropriate organs for excretion, such as the lungs, liver and kidneys. Carbon dioxide, which is produced by aerobic metabolism (*see* page 18) in mitochondria, is taken to the lungs to be exhaled. The liver is the main organ looking after detoxification, whilst the kidneys regulate water and the electrolyte balance.

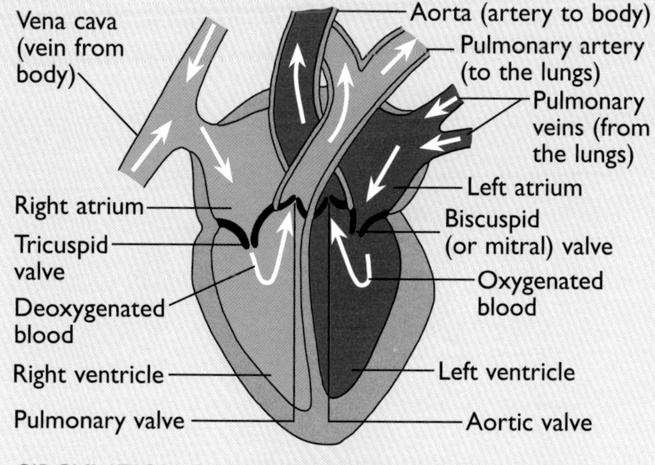

CIRCULATION OF BLOOD THROUGH THE HEART

What Does a Horse Need to Produce Movement?

To produce movement the horse only needs:

- A source of energy;
- Muscles to generate movement;
- Bones to support the body and for muscles to pull against;
- Joints so that bones can move and limbs can bend;
- Tendons to connect muscles to bones;
- Ligaments to stabilise the joints;
- A nervous system to tell the muscles when to contract, how hard to contract, and for how long to contract.

For roughly ten seconds of exercise, nothing else is needed, but the following extra components are required for longer periods:

- *A way of bringing oxygen to the muscles.* Oxygen allows the muscles to convert stored fuels (*see* page 16) into energy that the muscles can use.
- *A way of bringing fuels to the muscle.* Most glycogen in the body is stored within muscle cells but most fat is stored away from the muscle. Fat is important as an energy source for longer periods of exercise (more than 30 minutes) and so needs to be transported to the muscle. This is done by the circulation of the blood.
- *A way of removing waste products from the muscle.* Waste products build up during muscle activity (*contractions*).

The main waste products produced by the muscle are:

- *Heat.* Four units of energy are released as heat for every one unit of energy that is actually used to make muscles contract and generate movement.
- *Lactic acid.* Sometimes also just called *lactate*, lactic acid is produced during acceleration and at gallop when converting glycogen using oxygen cannot provide energy fast enough. Lactic acid is good in that it allows acceleration and fast running, but bad in that it limits the time the horse can work at speed.
- *Carbon dioxide* (CO_2). This is one of the major greenhouse gases in Earth's atmosphere, causing the temperature of the planet to rise. Carbon dioxide is produced by animals when glycogen and fat are 'burnt' to release energy. Carbon dioxide is also produced when fuels such as wood, coal, oil and gas are burnt in fires, engines, heaters or power stations.

Lactic Acid

Lactic acid is produced by the muscles when there is a need for rapid energy—such as during acceleration, running fast, and jumping. It allows for maximal effort, which is good, but if too much lactic acid is produced too quickly it will accumulate inside the muscle and lead to fatigue: this, however, protects the muscle from over-exertion and damage.

Producing energy with lactic acid is described as being 'anaerobic' because it does not need any oxygen. It is very fast but inefficient. To remove lactic acid requires oxygen. After a gallop the lactic acid is dissipated by the horse breathing heavily, or blowing. This is sometimes referred to as *repaying the oxygen debt*.

The longer and/or harder (faster) the horse is able to work without producing lactic acid (i.e. *aerobically*), the longer he will be able to work without becoming fatigued due to the accumulation of lactic acid. For horses who perform mainly aerobically—such as eventers, endurance horses, vaulting horses and carriage horses—fitness training should be aimed at encouraging the body to provide, and use, more oxygen. Horses competing in showjumping and mounted games, for example, will benefit from a mixture of aerobic and anaerobic training. Dressage is slightly unusual, as although in a test it would be unusual for a dressage horse to have a heart rate above 150bpm or an increased level of lactic acid in the blood, individual muscle groups may work anaerobically for short periods during particular movements. Generally, with aerobic training, as the horse becomes more aerobically fit it will be able to work at faster speeds, or for longer than an unfit horse, before its muscle cells begin to produce lactic acid.

Lactic acid removal can be important when horses or ponies are involved in repeated bouts of exercise: for example, one-day eventing, showjumping rounds, or mounted games. Lactic acid is removed more quickly at trot than at walk, and more quickly at walk than when standing, because increased blood flow aids the removal of lactic acid. *Warming down (see page 34) is an important factor in the dispersal of lactic acid.*

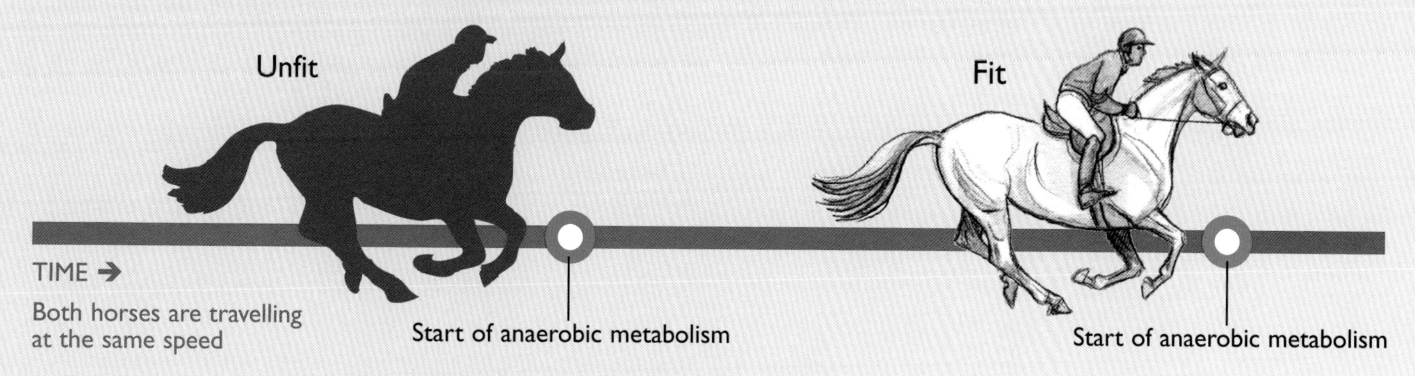

THE EFFECT OF TRAINING ON THE START OF ANAEROBIC METABOLISM
As the horse becomes fitter, the point at which anaerobic metabolism begins is delayed. The horse can work for longer before lactic acid is produced in the muscle cells, and the onset of fatigue is delayed.

Fuel

The only fuel that a cell can use—whatever kind of cell it may be—is ATP (*adenosine triphosphate*). Whilst plants can make energy from sunlight, *all of a horse's energy comes from his diet*. The energy stored in sugars, fats or proteins in foods eaten by a horse must be digested and converted into ATP before it can be used to make anything happen (including causing muscles to contract). Amazingly, muscles only contain enough ATP for two to three seconds of exercise, so as soon as muscle contractions begin, the processes that replenish the stores of ATP must instantly start working flat out. If they didn't, the horse would grind to a halt after a few seconds. (For convenience, from this point forward this book will just refer to fuel and energy, and not ATP.)

There are three different fuels that a horse can use during exercise, and the fuel used depends on the type of exercise, the duration of the exercise, and whether the horse is just starting exercise or has been exercising for some time. *Fats* (also known as oils, or lipids of free fatty acids (FFA)) and *carbohydrates* (sugars, glucose or glycogen) are the two main fuels. *Protein* can also be used as a source of energy, but this usually only happens during starvation, illness or sometimes in very prolonged exercise (such as endurance racing). For each gram of fat, there is much more energy stored than for a gram of sugar. The main sugar in animals is glucose. It circulates within the blood and is converted into long chains known as *glycogen*. Single units of glucose are able to move freely in and out of cells. In order to build up a store within the muscle cell some system of trapping the glucose units is required. When they are in chains they cannot move in and out of the cells. In plants, chains of glucose are known as *starch*.

Whether a short sprint or an endurance race, the fuel that is always limiting is glycogen. Even a thin endurance horse will have enough fat to complete two or three 100-mile races, but by the end of just one 100-mile race perhaps three-quarters of the muscle glycogen store will have been used up. In a five-furlong Thoroughbred sprint race, almost a third of the muscle glycogen store will have been used up. The amount of glycogen that is in the muscle also affects how fast it can be broken down to release energy. The bigger the store the faster the energy can be released.

Around 90 per cent of the glycogen in a horse's body is stored within the muscles and 10 per cent within the liver. The liver breaks down its glycogen stores and releases glucose into the blood circulation where it can be taken up by muscles and other tissues. Fat is different. Only around 10 per cent is stored within the muscles and 90 per cent is stored elsewhere in the body. Around eight to ten times as much energy is stored in the horse in the form of fat compared with glycogen.

Fats versus Sugars

The type of fuel that the muscles burn to generate energy for their use—and the way in which this fuel is burnt—depends on the type of exercise that the horse is doing.

Fat has a bad press but is actually great: when broken down with oxygen, one unit generates around four times as much energy as one unit of sugar! However, the release of this energy is twice as slow from fat as it is from sugar, and takes around half an hour to reach full speed (compared to two or three minutes for sugar).

The processes described above 'with oxygen' are referred to as being *aerobic* or, more accurately, *aerobic metabolism*. The combination of all the biochemical reactions that occur within an organism is known as *metabolism*. Metabolism takes place inside special structures inside the muscle cells (and in fact all living cells in the body except red blood cells) called *mitochondria*—which are often referred to as being a cell's 'power station'.

The Transfer of Energy

- Plants convert energy from sunlight into carbohydrates, fats and protein using photosynthesis using carbon dioxide taken from the air. Oxygen is released back into the air.
- The horse eats plants. Carbohydrates (sugars, glucose and glycogen), fats and protein contained in the plants are processed by the digestive system and released into the bloodstream—carbohydrates as glucose, fats as fatty acids.
- Oxygen from air inhaled by the horse enters the bloodstream in the lungs, and is then carried by the blood to the tissues.
- The stomach begins the digestive process.
- The small intestine converts carbohydrate into glucose.
- The liver detoxifies the blood. It processes protein, carbohydrate and fats; it also stores glycogen (10 per cent of the body's supply).

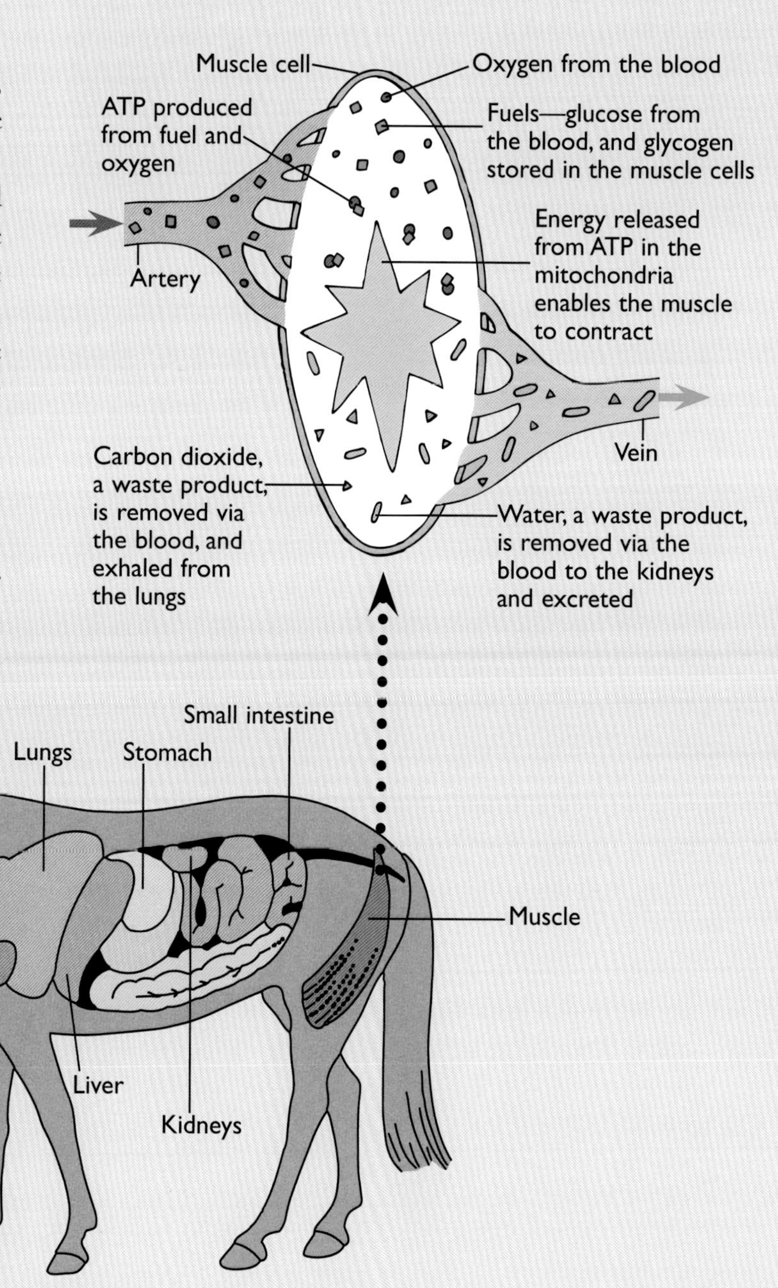

Aerobic versus Anaerobic

Aerobic means *with oxygen*, and *anaerobic* means the opposite—*without, or not needing, oxygen*.

Aerobic metabolism occurs when there is enough oxygen supplied by the blood to convert the glycogen stored in the cells into energy.

Anaerobic metabolism takes place when energy is needed quickly or when the horse is working very hard or when there is no longer enough oxygen left to convert glycogen into energy. This occurs when the horse is working at maximum speed; the muscle will then burn its glycogen reserves to produce energy without oxygen. Lactic acid is produced during anaerobic metabolism.

Aerobic metabolism of fat is very efficient and delivers energy slowly, but it takes a long time to get up to maximum supply. In comparison, *aerobic metabolism of glycogen* is less efficient—producing a quarter the amount of energy as fat—but delivers energy around twice as fast and also gets up to maximum supply more quickly.

- *Aerobic metabolism of fat* can be compared to a diesel engine (more efficient but with less performance);
- *Aerobic metabolism of glycogen* is more like a petrol engine (less efficient but with better performance);
- *Anaerobic metabolism of glycogen* can be compared to a rocket motor—because it gives high performance but doesn't last very long!

HOW THE DIFFERENT PACES AFFECT THE METABOLISM OF FUEL

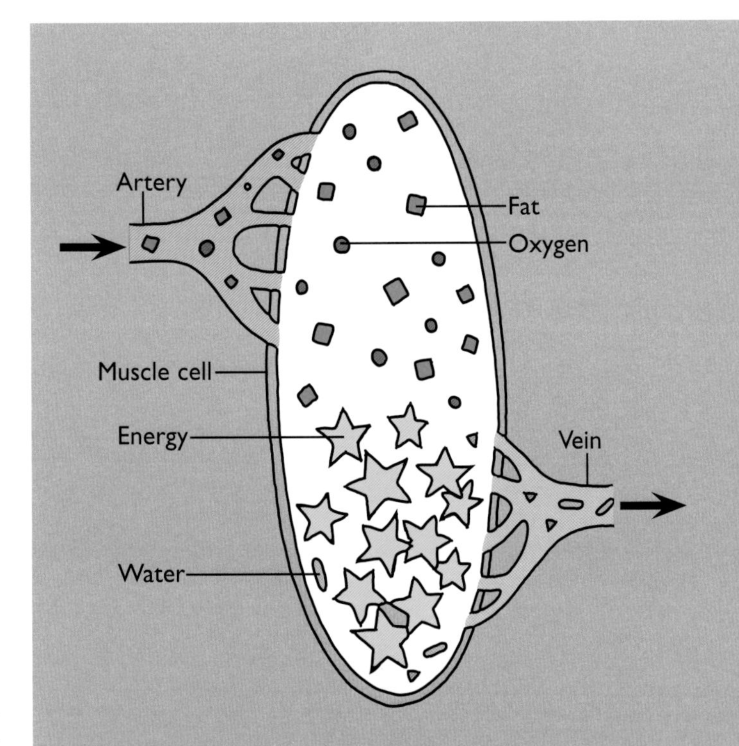

AEROBIC METABOLISM OF FAT
Energy production is slow but efficient (30 minutes to reach maximum speed)

TROT

Fat + oxygen,
glycogen + oxygen
AEROBIC

CANTER

Glycogen + oxygen
(fat + oxygen)
AEROBIC

GALLOP

Glycogen + oxygen,
glycogen – oxygen → lactic acid
AEROBIC + ANAEROBIC

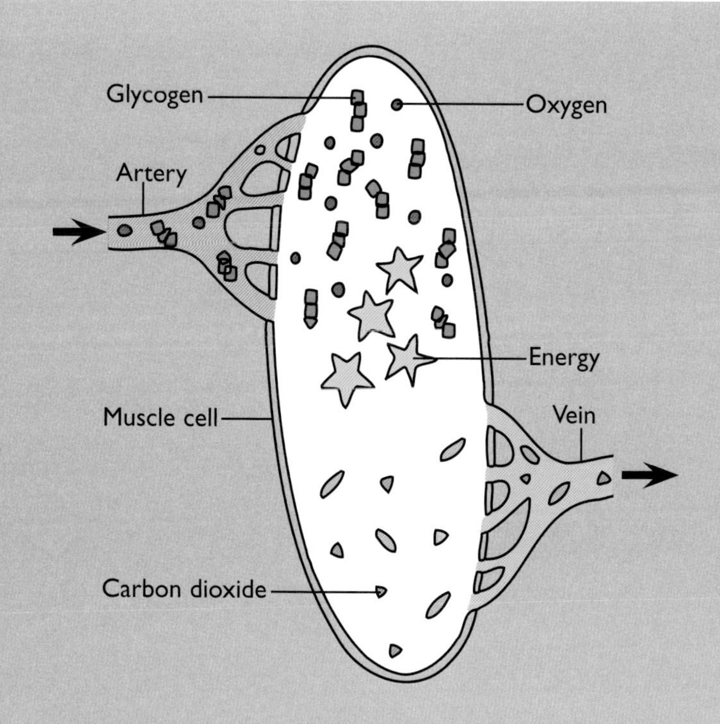

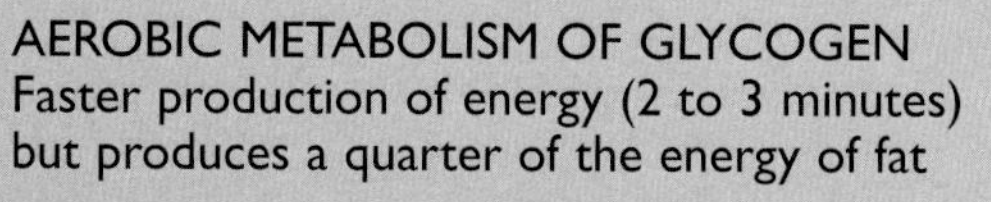

AEROBIC METABOLISM OF GLYCOGEN
Faster production of energy (2 to 3 minutes) but produces a quarter of the energy of fat

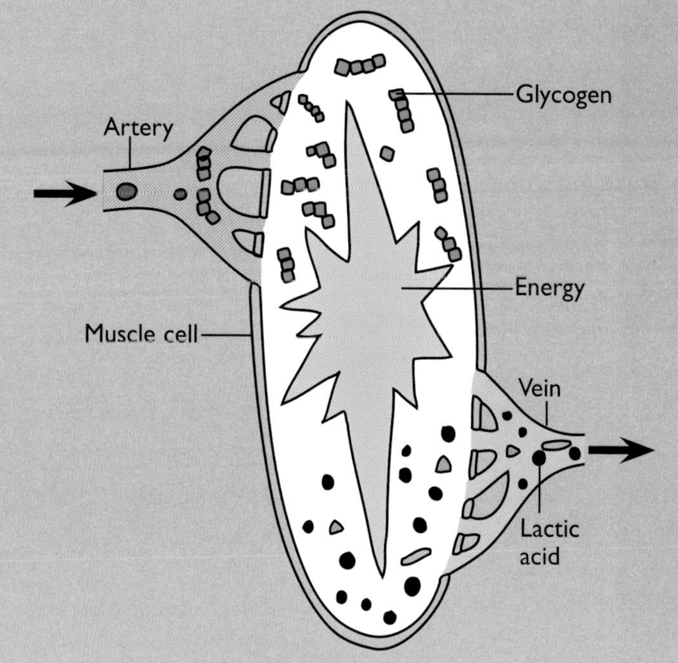

ANAEROBIC METABOLISM OF GLYCOGEN
Produces energy very quickly, but this does not last long. Lactic acid is produced as a waste product.

Changes to the Horse's Body During Exercise

How Does an Unfit Horse Respond to Exercise?

What could we expect to happen if a horse that had been turned out for three or four months was taken to a one-day event?

- *Poor performance.* There is every possibility that the horse may perform badly. This could be due to a combination of lack of physical fitness and a lack of skill-training.
- *Unnatural response to exercise.* At canter, horses normally take one stride with each breath. An unfit horse pushed hard may start to change his breathing or make unusual noises. He might sweat excessively or even collapse during or immediately after exercise.
- *Slow recovery.* Horses normally start to recover from exercise as soon as they pull up. After 5 to 10 minutes, their breathing is slowing and they start to look more comfortable and more alert. An unfit horse is likely to take much longer to recover after exercise and may *blow* (deep breathing) or *pant* (fast, shallow breathing) for a long time after exercise. He may also continue to sweat heavily and show little interest in eating or drinking.
- *Lameness.* Horses that have been over-extended for their level of fitness are more likely to suffer injury and may be seen to be lame as soon as they pull up.
- *Ataxia.* An unfit horse may be unsteady on his feet when he pulls up.
- *Reduced or greatly increased thirst and appetite.* The horse may show no interest in food or drink or may drink excessively.
- *Depression.* Depressed horses do not behave in the same way as normal ones. They show little interest in things going on around them. They may hang their head low, with their eyes half-closed. When you enter a stable, most horses that are lying down stand up, but a depressed or exhausted horse may not do so.
- *The morning after an event*, even if the pony or horse was fine at the finish, he may pull-out lame or stiff due to over-exertion.

How Does a Fit Horse Respond to Exercise?

- *Good, expected or acceptable performance;*
- *Normal response to exercise;*
- *Rapid recovery;*
- *Normal behaviour;*
- *Normal thirst and appetite after exercise and when back in stable.*

What Happens in the Body During Exercise?

The horse or pony's body is a complex machine with lots of different parts. Some, such as the muscles, are absolutely essential for exercise, whereas others, such as the reproductive system, play no part in it. Some have a role which lies somewhere between essential and non-functional. Some are still important for normal response to exercise but are not affected by exercise itself (such as the kidney).

There are three different types of muscle in a horse's body:

- *Skeletal muscle.* Used for movement and posture, this is the only muscle type in the body under voluntary control. It is therefore sometimes called *voluntary muscle*.
- *Cardiac muscle.* This is the muscle type that makes up the heart. The heart beats involuntarily and it is impossible for the horse to control its speed directly, although by thinking calm thoughts and relaxing the heart rate will fall.

- *Smooth muscle.* This is the type of muscle that moves food down the oesophagus and through the gut. It also lines the tubes in the lung and contracts when the airways are irritated (such as in asthma). It is not under voluntary control, and hence is also known as *involuntary muscle*.

What Happens in the Muscles?

Muscles generate movement by contracting (shortening). They are made up of thousands of small fibres between 3 and 300mm in length but each fibre is only 30 to 100μm across (μm is the abbreviation for micrometres, of which there are a thousand in every millimetre). The biggest muscle cells are only as wide as the average human hair (i.e. 100μm). The small and short fibres are found in muscles where fine movement control is needed, such as in the eye. The longer and wider fibres are found in the big muscles that are used for movement, such as the gluteal muscles (the muscles of the hind quarters).

When it comes to movement, we can ignore cardiac and smooth muscle and focus on skeletal muscle. There are around 700 different skeletal muscles in a horse or pony and they make up around half of the animal's weight. In very athletic breeds (such as the Thoroughbred), over half the body weight may be muscle.

Skeletal muscles can move on their own without our thinking about them: for example, the knee reflex where we tap the front of the knee and the leg jerks; or the reflex caused by an electric shock. But under normal conditions the horse or pony needs signals from the brain to make the muscles contract. He can decide when he wants to kick or run or move his head, and the appropriate signals are sent through nerves to the muscles to make them contract. The number of muscle fibres that a single nerve connects to depends on the function of the muscle. For the muscles of the eye and lip, for example, there may be one nerve for as few as ten to a hundred muscles fibres. For a big locomotory (running) muscle, there may be just a single nerve connected to several thousand muscle fibres.

When muscles are stimulated by a nerve impulse they contract. Contraction causes the tiny blood vessels in the muscles to open up (*dilate*) to allow more blood to flow through. The increased blood flow brings more oxygen and fuels (if needed for longer periods of exercise) and takes away heat, lactic acid and carbon dioxide. During exercise, muscles generate almost all the heat and are the reason why the horse must sweat and blow to try to control his temperature. The normal body temperature of a horse or pony is around 37°C but, during exercise, muscle temperatures may rise as high as 47°C.

After exercise, the blood flow to the muscle may be higher than normal for several hours until the muscle recovers. It may take from 24 to 48 hours for the muscle glycogen stores to become fully stocked-up. Minor damage may take the same sort of time to be repaired, but in the case of severe damage, it may take weeks or even months!

What Happens to the Heart?

The harder a horse exercises, the faster the heart needs to beat. This is why, as will be explained later on, measuring heart rate (*see* page 45) is the most practical way to assess how hard your horse or pony is working. The speed at which the heart rate recovers (*decreases*) after exercise or competition is a good indicator of fitness. When the muscles start to contract, the blood vessels in the muscles open up to allow more blood containing oxygen to flow into them. This also helps remove heat and other waste products. The heart must beat faster initially simply to maintain the blood pressure. The processes happening within the muscle also have an effect on the heart rate. The release of electrolytes, carbon dioxide, hormones and heat are all sensed by the brain and used to control the heart rate.

The Structure of Skeletal Muscle

Every muscle consists of millions of long, cylindrical cells—known as *muscle fibres* (also known as *myofibres*). They are arranged in bundles, which are held together by connective tissue. Each muscle fibre has several nuclei, which control the functions of the cell, and several mitochondria—which produce energy by breaking down glycogen or fats.

The nerves carry messages from the brain which stimulate the muscle to contract. The blood vessels carry oxygen and nutrients to the muscles; they also take away carbon dioxide, heat, and other waste products.

Each muscle fibre contains many *myofibrils*, and it is these myofibrils which contain the sliding filaments which enable the muscle to contract and relax.

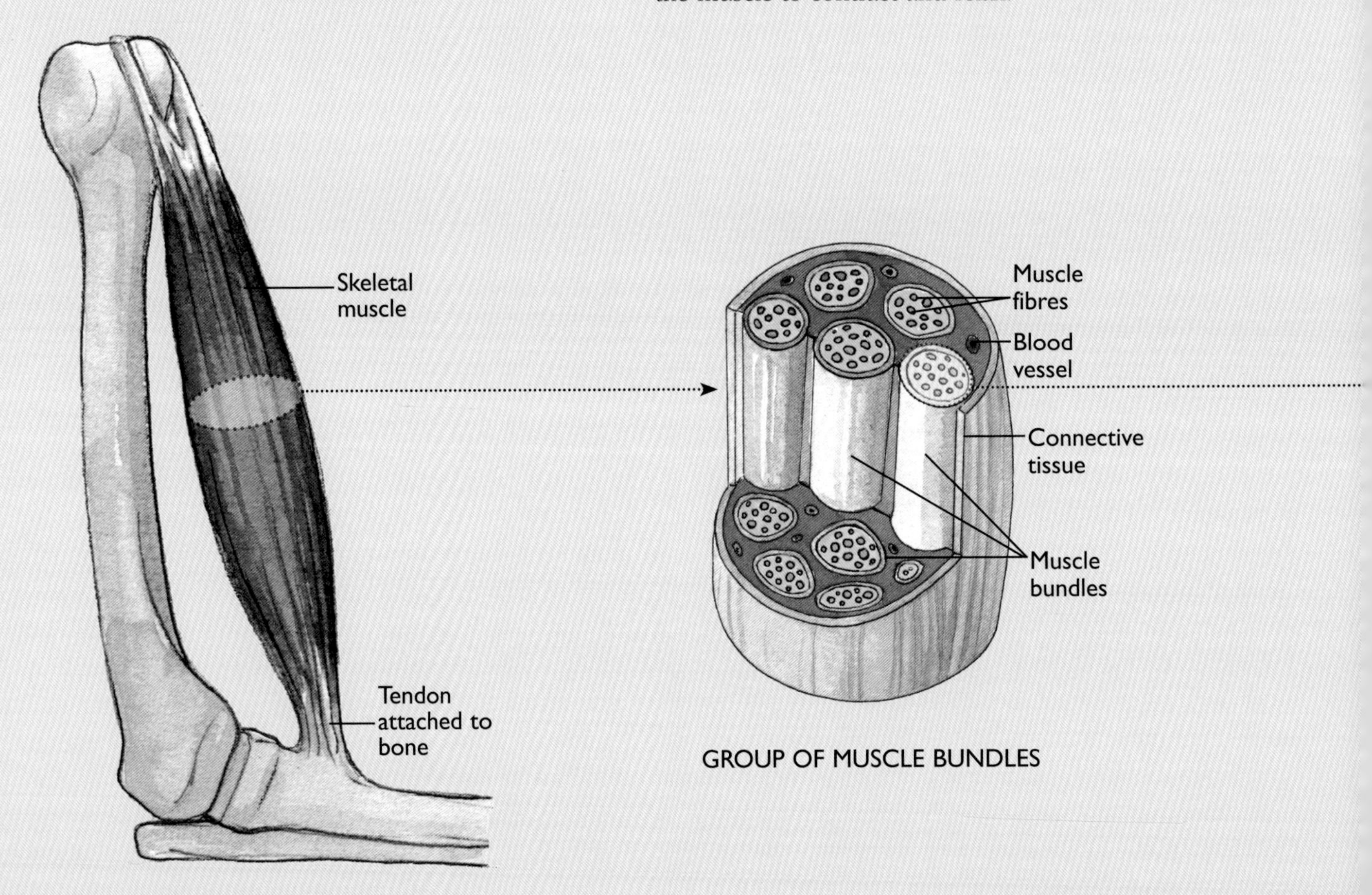

ENTIRE SKELETAL MUSCLE

GROUP OF MUSCLE BUNDLES

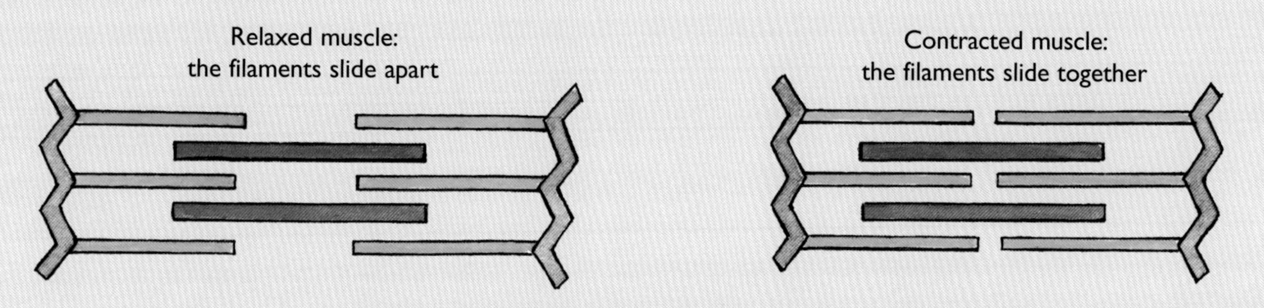

THE SLIDING FILAMENT MECHANISM OF MUSCLE CONTRACTION

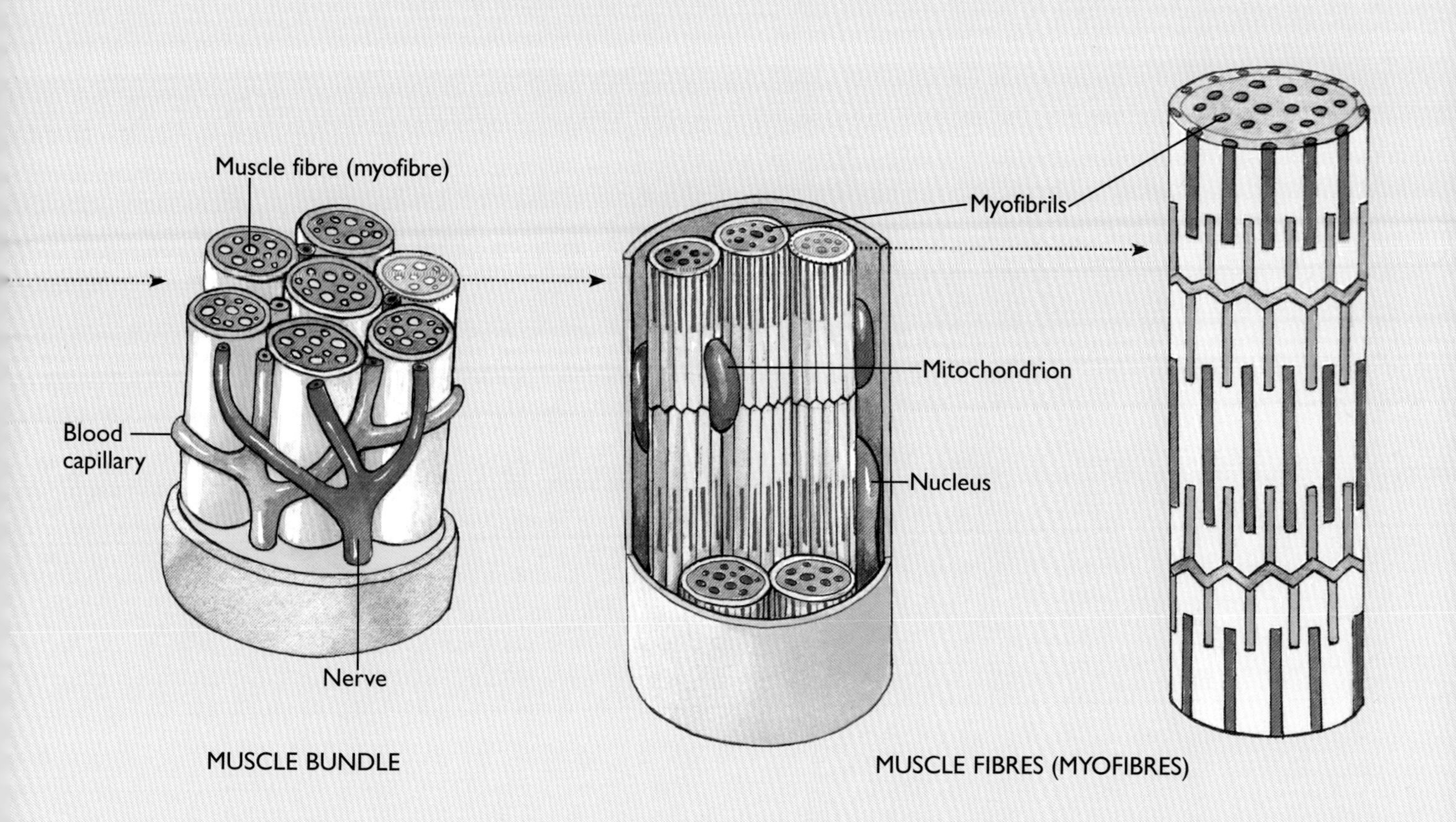

MUSCLE BUNDLE

MUSCLE FIBRES (MYOFIBRES)

Types of Muscle Fibres

Although we can't see it with our eyes, muscle is made up of thousands of fibres. There are two basic types of muscle fibre: *slow-twitch* (or *Type I*) and *fast-twitch* (or *Type II*).

Slow-twitch fibres are very red in colour as they contain higher amounts of *myoglobin*—a pigment which, like haemoglobin in the blood, stores oxygen; they rely heavily on oxygen to provide energy; and they therefore have many blood capillaries around them and many mitochondria inside them. This provides them with the capacity to generate large amounts of ATP by aerobic metabolism, which, as mentioned earlier, is very efficient but not fast-acting. These slow-contracting fibres are able to work for a long time without tiring, and are used for posture and when the horse is working slowly and continuously, requiring stamina rather than speed.

Fast-twitch fibres contract more quickly, are bigger, generate more force and are used for strength and speed. There are two types of fast-twitch fibres: Type IIb fibres are larger, faster-contracting, more powerful, and have fewer mitochondria in them and fewer capillaries around them. They rely heavily on anaerobic metabolism of glycogen (which produces ATP very quickly but rather inefficiently). The end-product of anaerobic metabolism is lactic acid. This allows the fibres to generate the explosive force needed for jumping, running flat out, or performing feats of strength; but it also protects the muscles from damage by limiting the time they can work at this level. Type IIa fibres are larger than those of Type I, but are generally smaller than those of Type IIb. They contain more mitochondria and myoglobin than Type IIb and can work for longer before fatiguing, but they also don't generate as much force as them. In a racehorse, the Type IIb and IIa fibres would contribute most to the race. In an endurance race, Type I and IIa fibres would contribute most. Type IIb fibres are also vital for jumping, accelerating, and running flat out.

The proportion of different types of fibres contained within a muscle is determined genetically and also according to where the muscle is in the body. Forelimb muscles usually have more Type I fibres, and hindlimb muscles more Type II fibres. The deeper you go in a muscle, the more Type I fibres you will find whilst, conversely, there are most Type II fibres near the surface of a muscle. Also, in training there

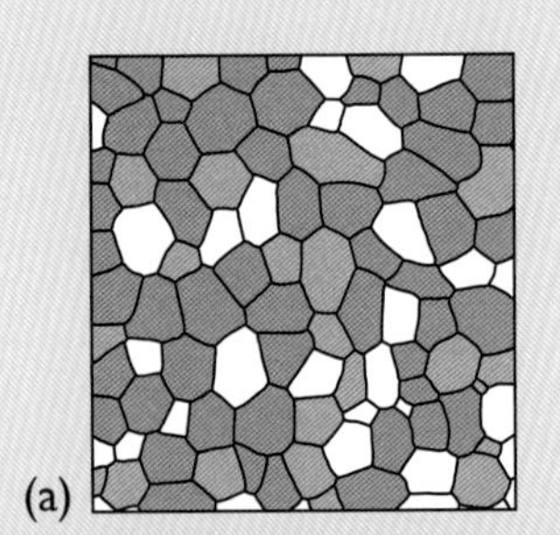

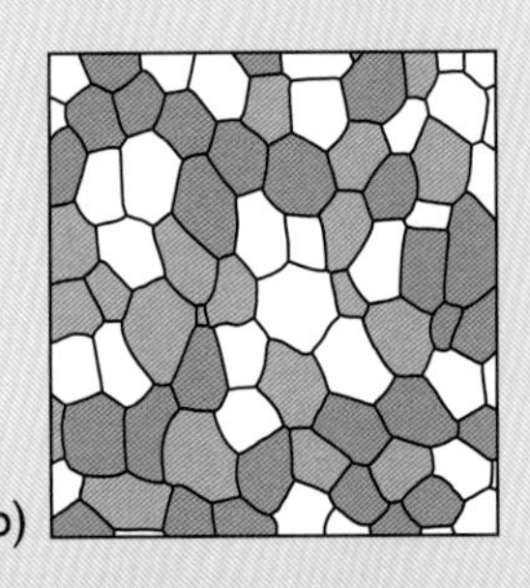

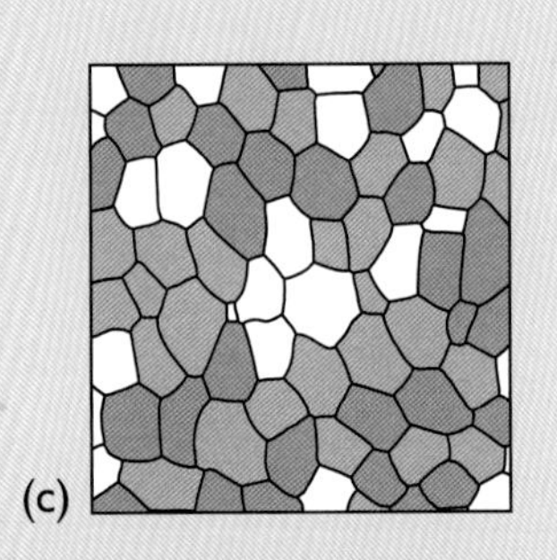

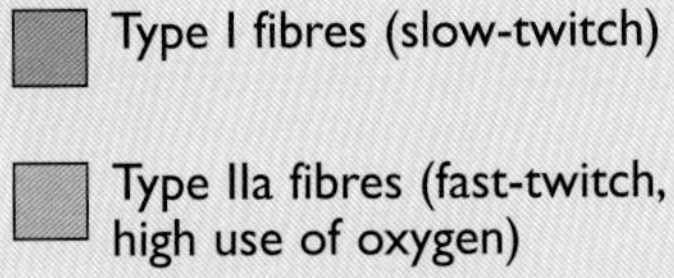

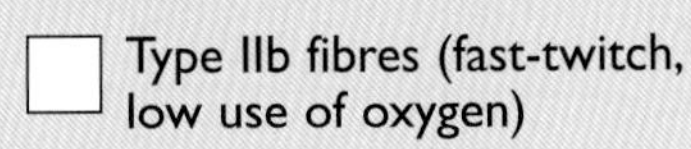

SKELETAL MUSCLE FIBRES SEEN THROUGH A MICROSCOPE
(a) Endurance horse: high percentage of Type I fibres
(b) Sprinting horse: high percentage of Type II fibres
(c) Sprinting horse after training: percentage of Type IIa fibres has increased

is an apparent change in the muscle fibres. It is not a real change—a Type I fibre will always be a Type I fibre—but with lots of fast sprint training it may start to take on the appearance of a Type II fibre. In the same way, concentrating on aerobic training may make many of the Type IIb fibres become smaller and have more capillaries around them and more mitochondria inside them. This will allow them to keep going for longer, generating more energy aerobically, but it will be at the expense of their power. A muscle fibre cannot be fast-contracting, powerful, and fatigue-resistant because the requirements for strength and speed are equal and opposite to the requirements for stamina. *A human athlete cannot be an élite marathon runner and also an élite sprinter!* The difference in appearance between sprinters and stayers in both horses and humans is due to differences in muscle fibre types. In general terms, fast breeds like Thoroughbreds will have more Type II fibres in their major locomotory (or running) muscles than, say, a hunter or a draught horse.

It is important to train correctly for the horse's chosen discipline in order to influence the development of the muscle fibres. A horse who is going to compete at speed, such as an eventer, must train at speed. An endurance horse must train at speeds that develop aerobic fitness: not at trot, and not at fast gallop!

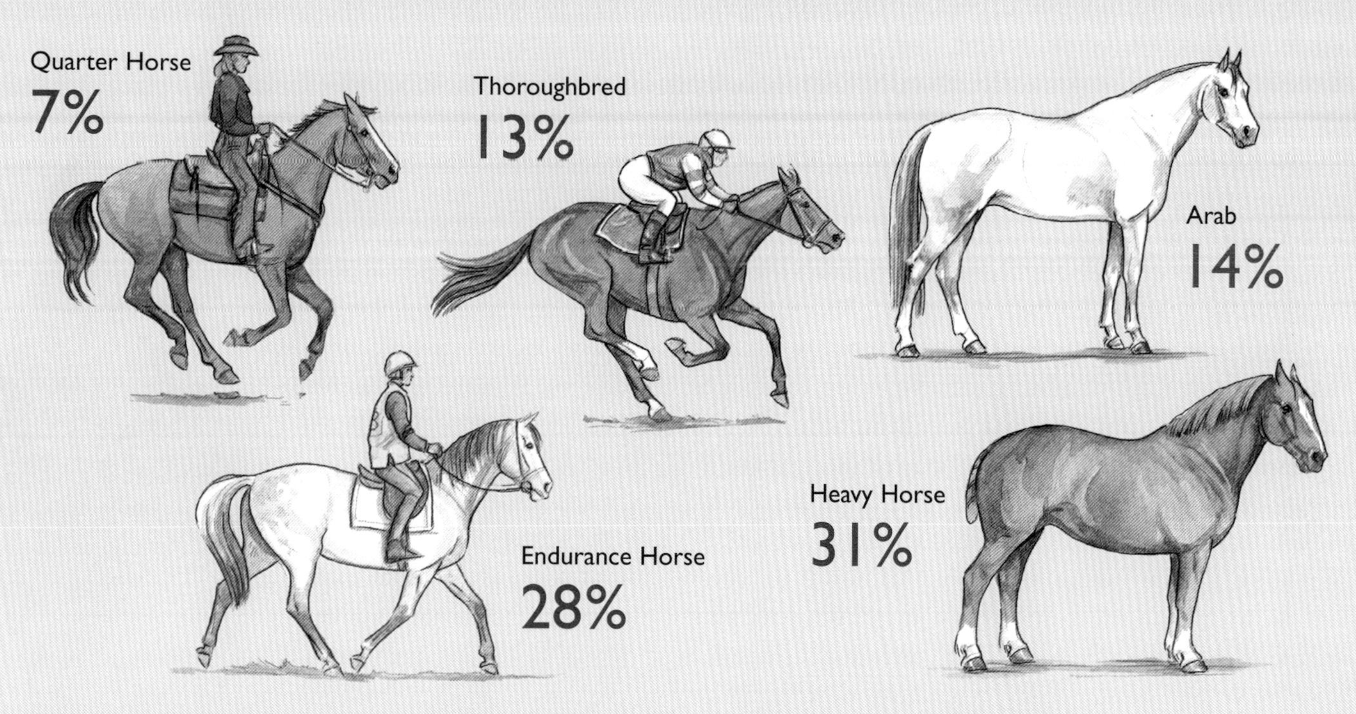

PERCENTAGE OF SLOW-TWITCH MUSCLE FIBRES IN THE MUSCLES OF DIFFERENT HORSES

What Happens to the Respiratory System?

The harder the horse works, the more oxygen he needs. Therefore the more oxygen he needs the more air must be moved in and out of the lungs for oxygen to be taken up by the blood and transported to the muscles where it is unloaded and used. The correct term for the process of moving air in and out of the lungs is *ventilation*. To eliminate carbon dioxide from the blood, ventilation must also increase as exercise intensity increases. So as oxygen moves from outside the body *in* to the muscle cells, carbon dioxide is going the other way—*out*.

At rest, an average-sized horse will take around twelve breaths per minute (this is known as the *respiratory rate*) or one complete breath—in and then out—every five seconds. Every breath moves around five litres of air in and out (known as the *tidal volume*), which is equal to the size of the average petrol container. Therefore, in one minute, the horse will move 12 breaths of 5 litres in and out, which comes to 60 litres in total!

During a fast gallop, an average-sized horse will move around 15 litres (roughly a bucketful) of air in and out *twice* every second, which means he is breathing 120 times per minute. The total volume of air moved in and out comes to 1,800 litres per minute, which is the same as six bathtubs full of air, or a bath being filled every 10 seconds (*see* opposite page).

A horse can increase his ventilation in three ways: by breathing faster (increasing the respiratory rate), by taking more air in (increasing the size of each breath), or by doing both.

From rest to walk, the horse increases his ventilation mainly by breathing faster, plus a small increase in the size of each breath.

From walk to fast canter, both the respiratory rate and the size of each breath are increased.

From fast canter to gallop, the increase in ventilation is mainly due to an increase in the size of each breath and there is little increase in the respiratory rate. This is linked closely to stride, with one stride to one breath.

The Link Between Breathing and Running

The horse's method of breathing is directly related to the gait, or pace, he is using. At walk and trot the horse's breathing does not work in time with the movements of the legs; his breathing and gait are *independent*. However, at canter and gallop his breathing and stride are perfectly *in time* and he takes a breath with every stride. This reduces the amount of energy used to breathe. When a horse has reached a fast canter (around 10 metres per second or 600 metres per minute), any further increases in running speed are made by taking longer strides—not by moving the legs faster. As the respiratory system is now linked perfectly in time with the legs, the only way the lungs can move more air in and out is by taking longer breaths. Breathing for longer allows the horse to take more in, so the size of each breath becomes larger but the number of breaths taken each minute stays the same. Overall the amount of air being moved in and out is increased.

Another important factor that affects breathing is heat. During walking and trotting, a hot horse will increase his breathing rate to help get rid of heat. At canter and gallop, because his breathing and stride are linked, he does not have this option. But when he stops exercising, if he has worked hard—especially in warmer weather—he will breathe very deeply and relatively slowly (around 60 to 80 breaths per minute). This is known as *blowing*, and the main purpose of it is to get rid of heat.

BLOWING GETS RID OF HEAT FROM THE HORSE'S BODY

RESTING HORSE

1 breath of 5 litres (10½ pints) every 5 seconds
12 breaths of 5 litres = 60 litres (13¼ gallons) every minute

1 BREATH

1 MINUTE

5 litres	5 litres
5 litres	5 litres
5 litres	5 litres
5 litres	5 litres
5 litres	5 litres
5 litres	5 litres

GALLOPING HORSE

20 breaths of 15 litres (3½ gallons) = 300 litres (66 gallons) every 10 seconds
120 breaths of 15 litres = 1,800 litres (396 gallons) every minute

1 BREATH

1 MINUTE

15 litres	15 litres	15 litres	15 litres	15 litres	15 litres	15 litres	15 litres	15 litres	15 litres	15 litres	15 litres	15 litres	15 litres	15 litres	15 litres	15 litres	15 litres	15 litres	15 litres
15 litres	15 litres	15 litres	15 litres	15 litres	15 litres	15 litres	15 litres	15 litres	15 litres	15 litres	15 litres	15 litres	15 litres	15 litres	15 litres	15 litres	15 litres	15 litres	15 litres
15 litres	15 litres	15 litres	15 litres	15 litres	15 litres	15 litres	15 litres	15 litres	15 litres	15 litres	15 litres	15 litres	15 litres	15 litres	15 litres	15 litres	15 litres	15 litres	15 litres
15 litres	15 litres	15 litres	15 litres	15 litres	15 litres	15 litres	15 litres	15 litres	15 litres	15 litres	15 litres	15 litres	15 litres	15 litres	15 litres	15 litres	15 litres	15 litres	15 litres
15 litres	15 litres	15 litres	15 litres	15 litres	15 litres	15 litres	15 litres	15 litres	15 litres	15 litres	15 litres	15 litres	15 litres	15 litres	15 litres	15 litres	15 litres	15 litres	15 litres
15 litres	15 litres	15 litres	15 litres	15 litres	15 litres	15 litres	15 litres	15 litres	15 litres	15 litres	15 litres	15 litres	15 litres	15 litres	15 litres	15 litres	15 litres	15 litres	15 litres

VOLUME OF AIR INHALED AND EXHALED

What Happens to Bone and Tendon?

During a single bout of exercise or competition there is very little change in bone. It does not have an increased blood flow nor does it get especially hot; and apart from supporting the body weight it has no other function. However, the load that is placed on bone is really the only signal which allows it to adapt to regular exercise by increasing in strength. Bone does require a certain amount of load to remain healthy and to be able to maintain its strength. However, if too much load is applied too quickly or too many loading cycles are applied (i.e. riding too far before the horse is ready), the bone may try to rapidly adapt. This is the process behind sore or bucked shins which are a sign that training is progressing too soon or too rapidly or both. One of the biggest risks of fracture in any horse is to train at *low loads* (e.g. walk and trot on soft surfaces) and then try to compete at canter and gallop on a hard surface (*high loads*). The bone will not be adapted to cope with the high load, and a fracture is a real possibility.

Tendon is mainly made up of elastic tissue and only contains a relatively small proportion of living cells. It also has very few blood vessels. This is partly why tendon injuries can take such a long time to repair. The fact that tendon is elastic means that when it is stretched and released it generates heat. You can prove this yourself by taking an elastic band and repeatedly stretching and releasing it: you will find that it gets warm. Similarly, with each stride, tendon is stretched and relaxed, generating heat. The more it is stretched (the faster the horse goes, the greater the stretch) and the more frequently it is stretched (the higher the stride rate) the greater the heat. The most heat is therefore produced during fast galloping or by cantering and jumping (jumping causes a high amount of tendon stretch both during take-off and landing). And because of poor blood supply, very little heat is removed by blood flow during exercise; the little heat that is released may be further decreased by the application of boots and bandages. This means that the highest temperatures within the body can be found in muscles and tendons.

What Happens to Other Organs?

Blood flow to organs such as the kidneys, liver and gut is reduced by exercise, and the harder the exercise, the more the blood flow is reduced. Though the gut is not necessary to support short duration exercise, it is important in endurance exercise for the supply of energy, water and electrolytes to prevent fatigue, dehydration and electrolyte-related problems such as tying-up or thumps. At low intensities of exercise the blood flow to the skin is increased in order to supply heat. This in turn results in production of sweat by sweat glands in the skin. The evaporation of sweat removes heat from the blood and cooler venous blood returns to the heart to be pumped back to the muscles. More heat is also removed as the blood moves through the lung and back to the heart before it is pumped out through the arteries to the muscles.

Training

What is Training?

In order to understand the nature of training and how to achieve it effectively, it is first necessary to define some terms:

- *Exercise:* activity or exertion that is usually planned and uses up energy above that at rest;
- *Training:* horses and ponies are trained so that they can cope more easily with tasks, such as exercise, and perform better; also because a trained (fit) horse or pony should be less likely to get injured or become ill after exercise. Training has several different functions:
  - To load into a lorry or horsebox;
  - To jump or do specific movements (e.g. extended trot)—sometimes referred to as *skill-training*;
  - To improve fitness—also referred to as *conditioning*.

  Skill-training can also lead to an improvement in fitness, and this is particularly true when a horse or pony is not very fit: for example, when coming back into work after a winter lay-off. Repeated flatwork sessions may also develop fitness, but as the horse or pony gets fitter, skill-training sessions may not be enough on their own to develop the level of fitness required for certain events.
- *Fitness:* the ability to cope physically with exercise;
- *Performance:* performance relates to what the horse or pony actually does in relation to a defined task—for example, jumping a course of jumps. *Good performance* would be a clear round, *poor performance* would be knocking three poles down.

The Goals of Training

- *To make horses easier and more enjoyable to ride;*
- *To decrease the risk of injury;*
- *To enable them to perform better.*

It has already been mentioned that there is a difference between training to improve skill and training to improve physical fitness, and it is important to recognise that though flatwork sessions may improve jumping or dressage movements, they may not result in any increase in physical ability to cope with exercise. In other words, they improve skill but not physical fitness. Training that results in increased physical fitness may make it easier for a horse to perform jumping or dressage movements or even movements required in mounted games. This in turn may lead to improvements in performance. In purely running events, such as flat racing or endurance racing, improvements in physical fitness may allow the horse to go faster or exercise for longer (improved stamina).

Repeated exercise sessions over a period of weeks or months are the essence of correct training and have a cumulative effect resulting in an increase in fitness and improved performance.

Three Key Points about Training

- *How often?* The exercise must be repeated frequently enough to get a response. A single fitness session, once a week, will not result in any improvement in physical fitness related to the bones, muscles or heart. On the other hand this does not mean that horses and ponies must necessarily be trained every day. Injuries to the muscles, joints, tendons and bones are common during training and lameness is the most common reason for a vet to be called to see a horse or pony. This suggests that horses and ponies are either being exercised too hard or too much.
- *How hard?* Generally, the faster we ride and the longer we ride, the harder the training session. But unfortunately it is a lot more complicated than simply speed and/or distance and/or time. There are many different factors that determine how hard a session of exercise will be for a horse or pony. The table on the right shows examples of factors that make exercise easy or hard for them. For example, exercising at canter uphill on a soft surface on a hot summer's day could be very hard work for a horse or pony.
- *What for? Speed, Stamina or Strength?* Human sprinters and marathon runners look very different. Sprinters are very well-muscled, whereas marathon runners are lean and slightly-muscled. This is partly due to the genes inherited from parents, but to some extent it is also a result of how they have trained. A sprinter will do a lot of strength and speed training while a marathon runner will focus on developing stamina. The key point here is that short, fast sprints and lifting weights make the muscles bigger and stronger at the expense of stamina which requires longer periods of exercise at moderate intensity. Stamina requires smaller muscle fibres with lots of blood vessels. Strength requires larger muscle fibres and few blood vessels. You cannot train to have maximum stamina *and* maximum strength: one will always

	LOW WORKLOAD	HIGH WORKLOAD
Terrain	Flat / downhill	Uphill
Speed	Walk	Gallop
Duration	Short	Prolonged
Surface	Hard	Soft
Environment	Cool	Hot
Altitude	Sea level	High altitude
Weight carried	Low	High
Pattern of exercise	Constant	Variable
Direction	Straight	Turning
Age	Young	Old
Ability	High	Low
Breed	Athletic	Non-athletic
Fitness	Fit	Unfit
Health	Good	Poor
Body Condition Score	Low / normal	High (i.e. obese)
Conformation	Good	Poor

be at the expense of the other. If you train for both—that is, half the time you focus on strength and speed, and half the time on stamina—you will end up as both a poor marathon runner and a poor sprinter! With horses and ponies the same applies. Think of the difference between a showjumper trained for speed and strength and an endurance horse trained for stamina. *If you want a fast pony for mounted games, don't do lots of long slow trotting work.*

Why Is It Easier to Get Some Horses Fit Than Others?

How a horse or pony copes with training will depend on the chosen programme but it can also vary between horses. You sometimes hear people say that a particular horse is *easy* or *difficult* to get fit. What might they mean by this? There could be two different reasons why a horse may be easy or difficult to get fit, and these reasons might seem surprising.

It may be that the horse in question is actually genetically very athletic: he has been born with genes that have given him all the ideal characteristics. When such horses and ponies are trained, they seem to cope very well with the work and appear much fitter than others, but this is actually misleading. They are coping with the work better because of their genetic make-up not because of their fitness. In fact, though appearing to perform better, these animals are likely to be not as fit as others around them and after a while the other horses may overtake them. Why? Because to a large extent the more difficult you find the exercise you are doing, the greater the training benefit. This is where the saying, '*No pain, no gain*,' comes from. While we don't want to take this too literally and make our horses and ponies hurt when we train them, it does mean that if they find the exercise too easy they won't get fit.

At the other extreme is the horse or pony who finds exercise quite hard. Because the exercise is hard for such animals they actually increase in fitness much more quickly than the more genetically-gifted animals. Initially they shoot ahead as far as fitness is concerned, but if the training of the more athletic horses and ponies is correct, then they will soon be overtaken.

How Long Does It Take to Get a Horse Fit?

This depends on a number of factors, including:

- Has the horse or pony been trained before?
- If previously trained, how long have they been turned out?
- Have they had paddock rest or box rest?
- How athletically-gifted are they?
- Do they have any health issues? (E.g. a previous tendon injury or tendency to go lame with work on hard ground.)
- What are they being trained for?

Age

As horses and ponies grow older they gradually become more aerobic (that is, better over longer distances as opposed to short, fast bursts). So for aerobic-type competitions (endurance, eventing) an older horse will have more of an advantage.

Previous Training

The general type of fitness training with horses and ponies makes them more aerobic. When a horse is turned out for a rest from competition or because of injury, there is a loss of fitness over several months. However, some of the changes that occur with training are retained so that when you bring the horse back in to work, he will not necessarily be back at the same level of fitness he had at the beginning of the previous season. (Bear in mind that sometimes it is difficult to separate the changes that occur with training from those that occur with age, as the two go together.)

Length of Time the Horse Has Been Off Work

Horses lose fitness very slowly compared with humans. A person who trains three to four times a week for twelve weeks and then takes a break of two to three weeks will be noticeably much less fit after the time-off than before it. But with a horse, after two to three weeks off work it would be hard to measure any actual physical change in his fitness. (There may, however, be changes in behaviour or skill that would mean that his performance was not as good.) It may well take four to eight weeks for a horse or pony with a high level of fitness to start to lose it, so even after a three-month lay-off he may not be back to square one as far as fitness is concerned.

One notable change that *can* take place without regular exercise is a loss of bone strength. Without daily loading (the weight of the body pushing down on the limbs at trot and canter) bone gradually starts to lose some of its strength. This will happen more with box rest than with paddock 'rest'.

Paddock Rest or Box Rest?

A horse in the paddock will do significantly more exercise and therefore retain his fitness for longer than a horse on box rest.

Talent or Genetics?

Most of a horse's athletic ability (as apart from his skills) is inherited. Training (fitness) actually only makes an improvement of 10 to 15 per cent. In theory, it should take the same amount of time to get a very athletic horse or pony fit as one who is less athletic, but in the early stages, if they are both unfit, a talented horse will have a greater capacity for exercise than a less talented one. As training progresses, their fitness should increase, and if they are trained as individuals the differences in their abilities should still be clear. However, if they are trained together the less talented horse may well catch up with his companion.

Health Issues

Horses who have previously had injuries should ideally be trained with them in mind, which may mean increasing the training load more gradually. Training on very hard or very soft ground should be avoided, so if conditions are not favourable it is better to miss a session than take a chance with a horse who has had orthopaedic problems (i.e. with bones, joints, muscles, tendons or ligaments).

What Are They Being Trained For?

Again, this applies to the physical fitness and not the skill. In general, the longer and more intense the type of competition that the horse is being prepared for, the longer the training programme required. It takes longer for horses to be prepared to compete in endurance and eventing than in showjumping, because a horse is more naturally a sprinter than an endurance athlete.

What Happens When We Start Training a Horse?

By repeating the right sort of exercise frequently enough, a horse's body will adapt over time and there will be an increase in fitness, which should improve performance and decrease the risk of injury. Training the wrong way, however, can cause the horse to be lame, resulting in little or no increase in fitness.

Most training programmes start with several weeks of walking and trotting, followed by gradually building up the distance and speed. At this point it is very important not to get bored and impatient and decide to fit in a 'quick gallop'. The horse or pony's bone and tendons will not be prepared for this, and an injury is a high risk. The muscles are also unlikely to be ready and so there is also a high risk of a strain. Possibly even worse is that weak muscles may lead to the horse placing a foot wrongly and stumbling or tripping—or even lead to a tendon injury.

In the next phase, after two to three weeks of long, slow, distance work, the speed is increased by starting to canter. Initially this may be for short distances, two or three times a week. The horse or pony can also be doing some flatwork training in an arena or in the paddock. It is important to remember that although flatwork training is necessary for suppleness and for settling the horse and developing skill, it is not a replacement for the type of exercise that will promote fitness. Generally, though some muscles may be working quite hard at certain stages of a flatwork session, this does not equate to the effort of a fitness session. During the first four to six weeks, most of the changes to the heart and muscle that increase the aerobic capacity will have taken place. In an unfit horse, the main system that limits how much exercise can be done is the circulatory system (heart, blood vessels and blood). After training, it is the respiratory system: the reason being that the heart is a muscle and can adapt to training. The respiratory system does not change as a result of training: nor do tendons get stronger.

Bone will strengthen as a result of increased loading, but, to become strong enough to cope with cantering and galloping, the bone needs to be prepared. It will only adapt to what it is being exposed to, and this is why speed must be increased gradually and not suddenly.

In the third and final training phase, more speed work is usually included. This may involve increasing the speed and canter and then adding in some gallop sessions. If each of these phases is planned correctly (i.e. the right number of exercise sessions per week over the right distance and at the right speeds) probably 90 per cent or more of the horse or pony's fitness development will have been completed in ten to twelve weeks. This is also based around three to four fitness sessions a week and an increase in the speed and/or distance every ten to fourteen days.

As the horse becomes fitter through regular training, it will find exercise and competition easier and will recover more quickly.

Competitions Do Not Get Horses Fit!

It is not competitions but regular and repeated bouts of exercise (training) which get horses fit, and once fit it is likely that competing three times a week may be enough to maintain their fitness. After training six days a week for ten weeks (*sixty exercise sessions!*) one single competition makes virtually no impact on your horse's fitness; he may need the competition for experience, but that is not the same thing as needing it for fitness.

Excess Weight

If your horse or pony has been at pasture for a break and is overweight, this is not the ideal condition in which to start hard training. Excess weight means excess stress on muscles, tendons, bones, ligaments and joints. It would be better to reduce the weight before starting serious training.

Surfaces

All horses and ponies have to be trained on a surface of some kind, and the golden rule is to try to use the best surface available. Avoid uneven and very deep surfaces. Roads are not very satisfactory and the belief that they 'harden up' tendons is a myth. Hard surfaces will not help tendons; are likely to lead to an increased risk of joint problems; and are often slippery for shod horses. However, sensible roadwork has a place as part of hacking out for education, fitness and pleasure.

Planning

Plan your training programme and stick to it. Don't be tempted to add some extra sessions. Calculate on the calendar when you want your horse to be fit and then work back twelve weeks. You should be able to get a horse fit in ten, but the extra two weeks allow for unforeseen problems: you sprain your ankle; you go down with flu; your horse gets a saddle sore; the ground is frozen, etc.

Tack

Having a rider on board can create problems for a horse or pony in three main areas. Firstly, the mouth (through the rein contact). Secondly, from the extra weight being carried (and its effects mainly on the legs). And last but not least, the area where you are almost in direct contact between the saddle and the horse. The horse or pony will change shape as he gets fitter, and this can be quite dramatic if he was overweight to start with. A saddle that fits well in the first week of training is unlikely to fit as well in week ten, so it is worth checking out the fit when you are nearly at the end of your fitness training.

Warming Up

We all know that we should not go from sitting down watching television to running flat out. It is likely to damage a muscle at the very least. The same applies to horses, and any exercise session should start with easy walking, gradually taking up the reins and making the horse walk more actively, then progressing into trot. At least ten minutes of walk and five minutes of trot should be used as a warm-up, not forgetting to change the rein.

Warming Down

A period of warm-down is important, especially if a horse or pony is visibly sweating or his breathing is fast and shallow, or slow and deep, which indicate that his body temperature is significantly above normal resting temperature.

Watering

Horses and ponies are usually thirsty when they finish work. Tradition has taught that they should not be allowed to drink, yet recent experience has shown that it is perfectly safe and, in fact, desirable to allow them to drink at least half a bucket of water immediately after exercise—even when they are still blowing and/or sweating and before they have recovered.

How Often—and When—You Should Train

The minimum for getting a horse or pony fit is three exercise sessions in a seven-day period which should ideally be equally spaced. It is much more effective to train on a Monday, Wednesday and Friday than on a Friday, Saturday and Sunday. The problem with training over a weekend is that the horse gets no chance

How Fat is Too Fat?

The climate in Great Britain confronts our horses with a *feast or famine* situation: rich grazing in spring and summer, followed by bare mud in the winter. A horse living in the wild would cope with this by putting on enough weight in the summer to enable survival through harsh winter conditions. However, our domesticated animals are well-fed all year round and often don't lose extra weight gained in the summer. This can develop into a real problem, with horses and ponies becoming seriously and chronically (i.e. long-term) overweight over a period of years. Obesity carries serious health risks for horses (just as it does for humans). Not only does it put extra stress on the various structures and systems of the body—particularly joints and tendons—but the overweight horse also runs an increased risk of becoming laminitic. Obese horses are also more lethargic and less willing to work.

A very effective method to tell if your horse is overweight is to use *Body Condition Scoring* (see pages 36/37), which allows you to assess the amount of body-fat your horse is carrying without the need for scales or weigh-tapes.

to recover. A small problem that occurs on a Friday may be a big problem by Sunday night. The lack of training between Sunday and the next Friday also means that a lot of the benefit of the previous weekend has been lost due to lack of stimulation of the heart and muscles. And as all the exercise is concentrated into three days, the risk of injury is greater. In the winter many people will be restricted to riding at the weekend because of school or work during the week and because it gets dark so early. The problem is that training only on a Saturday and Sunday is not effective.

A training programme that will maximise fitness and decrease the risk of injury involves fitness work for two days in a row, followed by a day off from it (which could involve flatwork or jumping), then another two days of fitness work... and so on. Unfortunately this does not tally with the normal seven-day week, so a compromise would be two days fitness, one day flatwork, two days fitness, one day flatwork, one day turnout.

Stepping Up the Work

Plan to step the work up to the next level every ten to fourteen days. The reason for this is that the horse's body adapts quite quickly to the right kind of exercise and after eight sessions will be ready to move up to the next level. But it is important not to make the steps too big. If the horse is walking for ten minutes, trotting for twenty minutes, and walking for ten minutes, don't step up to walking ten minutes, cantering twenty minutes, walking ten minutes. More appropriate would be walking ten minutes, trotting ten minutes, cantering five minutes, trotting five minutes, walking ten minutes.

Recovery Weeks

It is very useful to include recovery weeks in a training programme. These are used by human athletes but not very often in horse exercise programmes. The idea is simple: you train for, say, two weeks; then drop the work down for a week; increase for two weeks; then drop back a week.

Tapering

Most riders do more with their horses or ponies as they get close to a competition. This is the complete opposite to human athletes who actually do less training as they approach a competition. This is known as *tapering* and has been shown to improve performance in both human athletes and horses. The reason is actually quite simple. Daily training, even for fit animals without any injury, causes some muscle damage and uses up some of the energy stored in the muscle. A period of tapering allows the muscle to repair any damage and restore the energy reserves, and both of these things contribute to increased muscle strength, endurance and performance. In order to taper before a competition, starting about seven to ten days before you would normally train your horse or pony, gradually reduce the amount of exercise time each day. Do the same type of exercise each day (speed and gaits), but progressively less and less of it (time at each speed or gait).

How Do You Know When Your Horse is Fit Enough?

If your horse or pony is fit and healthy enough for a competition, he should be able to cope with what you are asking without signs of distress or over-exertion. This means he should not have an irregular stride; stumble frequently; appear excessively tired; or feel unsteady. After competing, the horse or pony may be hot and tired but he should not become unsteady on his feet when pulled up and he should not appear agitated or distressed in any way. After being allowed to cool off, or cooled off with water (or in warm weather with ice and water), within ten minutes or so he should be showing signs of recovering from the exercise.

Body Condition Scoring

Assess your horse visually and by running your hands over his body. Compare what you see and feel with the illustrations and text on this spread. Ideally, your horse should not score less than 2 or more than 3. Bear in mind that certain conformation factors—such as high withers or a flat back—may affect the score, making it appear lower than it really is.

If your horse is scoring 4 or 5 you should think very seriously about how you are going to help him lose weight. Increasing exercise, removing concentrates from the feed (but adding a good vitamin/mineral supplement or balancer) and calculating carefully the amount of feed and hay you are giving are all good ways of helping him slim down. Grazing should also be restricted by cutting down turnout time, strip grazing, or fitting a muzzle. Aim for the horse to lose weight slowly and safely.

0 Very Poor

Backbone, ribs, hipbones and tailhead all project. Bone-structure of withers, shoulders and neck easily seen. No fatty tissue can be felt. Horse is emaciated. Three bony processes of each vertebra can be felt.

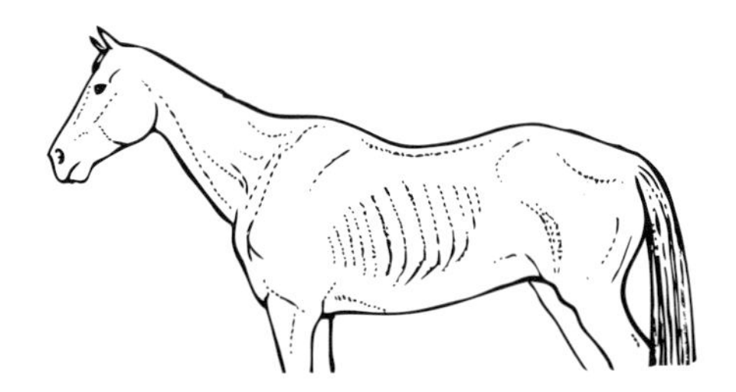

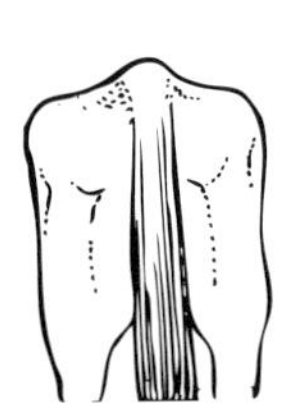

1 Poor

Bones of the neck can be felt. Slight covering of fat. Slight covering of muscle over the join of the neck and shoulder. Withers are prominent. Slight covering of fat over ribs, but ribs still visible. Upper (spinous) process of vertebrae can be felt: two transverse processes have a slight covering of fat. Bones of the tailhead project.

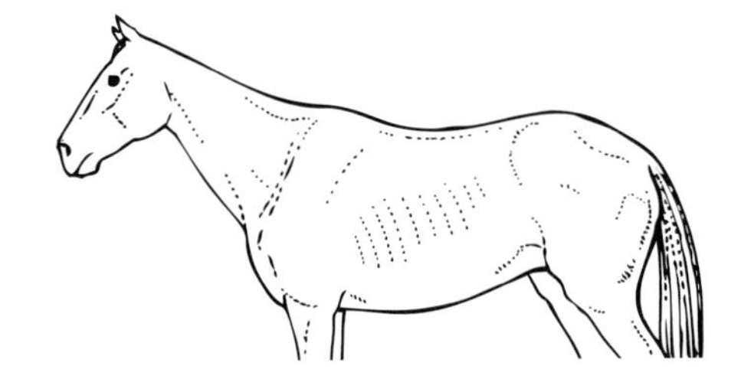

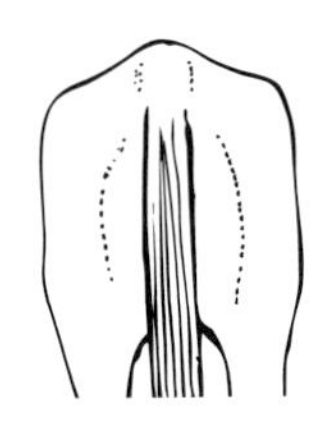

2 Moderate

Neck, withers and shoulders have a covering of fat. Ribs are barely visible, but can be felt. The spine and hip bones have a covering of fat. The vertebrae have a covering of fat: spinous processes not visible.

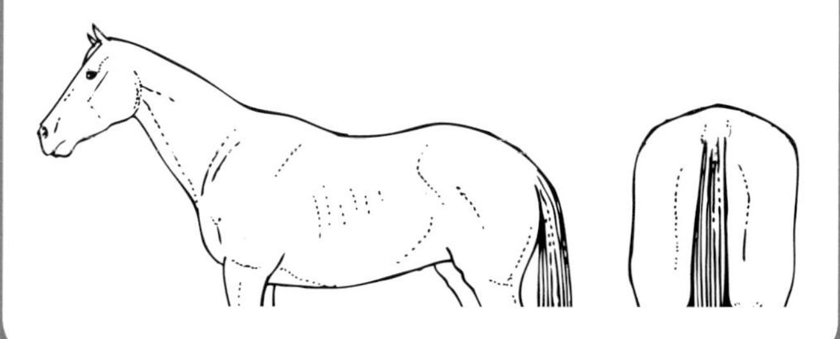

4 Fat

Spongy fat over and between ribs. Fat deposits along withers, behind shoulders and on neck. Fat around tailhead is soft. A crease can be seen running down back. Slight crest on neck. Withers losing definition.

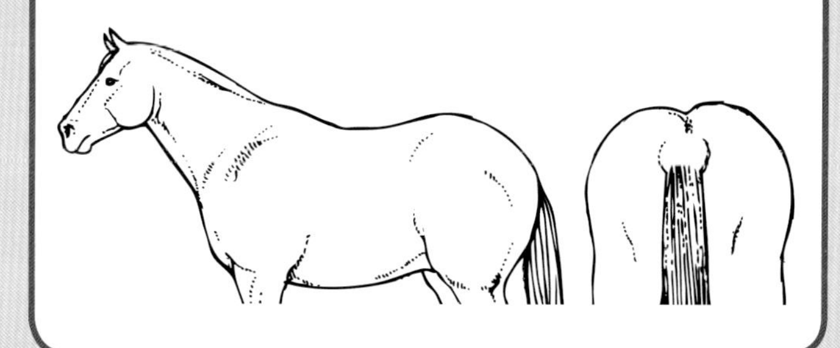

3 Good

Neck runs smoothly into shoulder. Neck rounds out of withers: shape of withers still visible. The back is level. Hip bones cannot be felt. Ribs have a covering of fat.

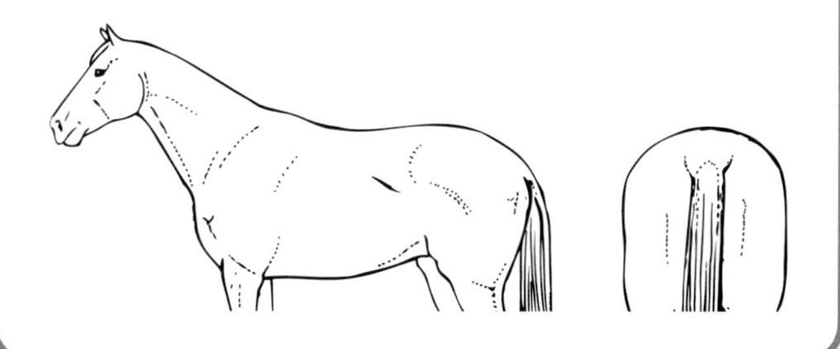

5 Very Fat

Obvious crease down back. Fat in patches over ribs. Bulging fat over tailhead, withers, neck and behind shoulders. Structure of withers not visible. Inner buttocks may rub together. Flank is flush with barrel of body. Pronounced crest.

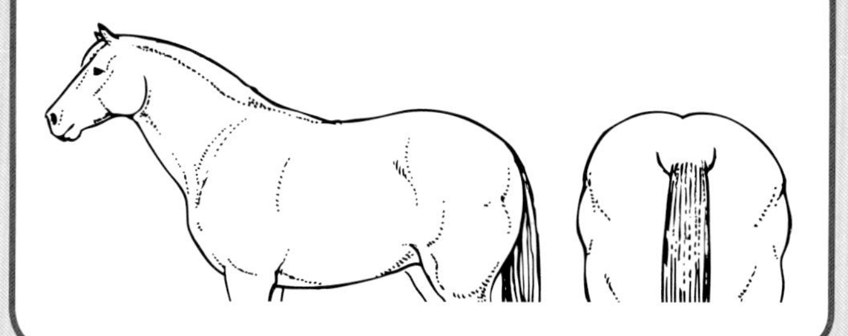

Training and Fitness for Different Disciplines

ENDURANCE

Endurance horses are the marathon runners of the equine world. At the highest level they are examples of superbly-fit athletes with body-fat as low as 5 per cent (which is similar to their human counterparts).

The rider also needs to be extremely fit in order to avoid causing injury (to the soft tissues under the saddle) through not supporting their own body weight and maintaining balance. Fitness and strength in the rider is also important for sitting squarely: unbalancing the horse by sitting unevenly over long periods of riding can cause injury to both rider and horse.

Endurance horses will benefit from an initial two to four weeks of long, slow work—building up gradually. There is no benefit to pounding the roads, as this only leads to wear and tear and the risk of falls, and does not 'harden' tendons. As cantering is introduced, the amount of work at trot can be reduced. The work at canter can be increased in both time and speed until the horse or pony is able to work comfortably at a fast canter for 10 to 15 minutes after 12 to 16 weeks of training. The important points are to try not to push the horse too hard and to increase the work gradually. If you want to compete in rides over hills, then you should train your horse over hills. If you want to enter rides on flat courses, most of your training should be on the flat.

DRESSAGE

The training of a dressage horse has three components:

- *The relationship between rider and horse;*
- *Skill* (the horse must learn to perform the movements);
- *Fitness.*

Dressage movements are undertaken at relatively slow speeds and at low heart rates (less than 150bpm). This

would normally lead us to conclude that dressage is aerobic, and on a whole-body level that is true; but particular movements, especially many of the more advanced ones, are *anaerobic* and rely on strength and power rather than stamina (aerobic capacity).

The mental attitude of the horse is very important. He must accept training and discipline without fighting or resisting. Through training, the horse becomes more collected: his centre of gravity moving backwards as the hind legs engage underneath the body and he comes off of his forehand. This can take some years to achieve. Muscle tone is slow to build up but can be lost fairly quickly, which needs to be given consideration when thinking about long periods of turnout. On the other hand, once horses are fit, less work is needed to maintain the fitness than is needed to get them fit in the first place. When there are no competitions or when the weather is unsuitable, periods of reduced work are perfectly acceptable, as are longer periods of turnout for two to three weeks. During this period very little fitness will be lost. Although the horse can develop adequate fitness for dressage by working in the school, hacking will be of benefit psychologically as well as physically.

SHOWJUMPING

Showjumping is a speed and power discipline, and there is no requirement for stamina because jumping-rounds usually last for only one or two minutes. There is little need for long, slow work which will increase stamina. However, it is important to start with short periods of jumping and flatwork, and to build up gradually to allow the bones to adapt to the increased load. Jumping requires a skill component and a fitness component. Human athletes who jump, such as hurdlers, will normally train using a combination of methods to develop skill and

to increase muscle mass. Just as for disciplines requiring development of stamina, development of speed and strength will take many months. Flatwork will help develop balance and collection and will improve the paces, particularly the canter. A young horse will need to be trained over jumps more often than an older, more experienced horse. All training for jumping should begin with around 15 minutes at walk, trot and canter to get the horse properly warmed up. As with the dressage horse, hacking will be of benefit, helping with fitness and preventing the horse becoming bored and stale.

The horse that specialises in speed jumping should be trained in fast work to develop anaerobic capacity; this should include some fast canter and short gallop work. As the height of the fences increases and as the horse's career progresses there should be less focus on speed and more focus on strength training.

EVENTING

Getting the horse fit for eventing presents some potential problems for the rider or trainer. The event horse is considered by some to be the ultimate all-round athlete: he must be calm and supple enough to do a dressage test; fit enough and brave enough to gallop and jump across country; and obedient and careful enough to complete a course of show jumps. This is a lot to ask, as we have already seen that the physical requirements of each of the phases is very different—demonstrating that training the event horse is a compromise. Obviously, schooling in the three disciplines of cross-country, showjumping and dressage must be included in the eventer's training but, as with all other fitness programmes, the basis consists of three to four weeks of slow work. After this initial period the amount of slow work can be gradually reduced as faster work is introduced.

The horse should be worked in gallop at speeds that he will be required to do a cross-country, and he must learn to be calm and balanced and to lengthen and shorten his stride. He will need to practise cantering up and down hills and inclines if he is going to encounter these in actual competition.

Interval training is sometimes used by event riders as a way of getting the horse fit enough to compete, and it has two advantages. The amount of work that can be achieved by doing, for example, four lots of one-minute gallops is essentially the same as one single four-minute gallop. The difference is that four lots of one-minute are more effective in increasing fitness and at the end of each one-minute lot the horse is not as fatigued as at the end of a single four-minute gallop, reducing the risk of injury. Interval training consists of giving the horse timed and measured periods of canter or gallop work followed by short recovery periods in walk. For example, a two-minute gallop to the top of a field and a five-minute walk back to the start. The aim of this method is to increase progressively the horse's capacity to work at speed. Whilst it is effective it does not suit all horses' temperaments and some horses become over-excited by the repetition.

An essential element in this training system is the monitoring of the horse's temperature, pulse and respiration (*see* pages 43 and 45). After one interval, and before the next, the horse should show clear signs of recovery. Having a heart rate monitor is the easiest way to check the horse's heart rate. During the canter or gallop phase the heart rate should be over 170bpm. As the horse pulls up, the heart rate will drop rapidly to around 120 to 100bpm, and in a fit horse, as a rule of thumb, it should be below 100bpm in one minute. If the horse is still blowing, has a high heart rate (greater than 90bpm) and/or it is still sweating heavily when it is time to start the next interval, this is a sign to STOP!

POLO

Polo is a very demanding sport for the pony—both physically and mentally. Although each chukka lasts only seven minutes, the pony is on the go from beginning to end, with constant changes of speed and direction. Basic fitness comes first: three to four weeks of walk and trot as for most ridden horses. Then the pony should be schooled with the focus on speed and agility—stopping and starting, change of leg, and turns on the haunches. The pony should also be worked in canter. After six to eight weeks of training, short intervals of sprinting (50 to 100 metres) will help to develop speed and power. Training in the movements and pattern of exercise that the pony will use when competing will encourage the development of the right kind of muscle fibres.

FLAT RACING

In the wild, a horse spends most of its time walking, occasionally trotting (to show off or play) and galloping when startled or excited. Very little time is spent cantering. So the most frequently used gaits for the wild horse are walk and gallop. Even though with conventional training programmes horses spend most of their time cantering in training, races are, of course, run at the gallop. Most of a racehorse's ability is there from day one and is determined by the genes that it has inherited from its parents. The improvement that training adds to performance is surprisingly small—perhaps as little as one-tenth! However, training is also important as it should reduce the risk of injury. For example, an untrained horse's bones will be less dense, and therefore less strong, than those of a trained horse. Thus, galloping any horse when unfit carries an increased risk of a fracture.

Races vary in distance from 5 to 20 furlongs (1,000 to 4,000 metres), and each horse will have its own favoured distance, which is also determined at birth by the genes it has inherited. The fitness programme must be carefully tailored to suit each race that the horse runs, bringing it to peak fitness on the day of the race. This should involve tapering. As with any training programme, increases in work should be made slowly and gradually, avoiding sudden changes, such as going from a baseline of trot to fast canter or slow canter to gallop.

MOUNTED GAMES

These ponies need to be obedient, supple, and above all, *fast*, and their training should consist of work that helps to develop these qualities. They must be able to accelerate to full speed from a standing start. Plenty of short sprinting work (intervals) over short distances (50 to 100 metres) will help develop the Type IIb muscle fibres that provide power for sprinting. Flatwork exercises that focus on suppleness and obedience will also be of use. Ponies who are overweight will be at an increased risk of injury and will not perform as well.

Effects of Training on the Horse's Body

Muscles

Aerobic training enables the muscle cells to use energy more efficiently. It also increases the availability of fuel to the muscle fibres by encouraging the development of more mitochondria and enzymes which break down glycogen and fat to supply energy. The blood supply is increased as the number of capillaries around each muscle fibre (cell) increase, giving a greater supply of oxygen. The muscle fibres also store more glycogen, and the ability to use fat as an energy source is improved, especially if fat is fed in the horse's diet.

In a horse trained for strength—such as a dressage horse—the muscles will increase in size as the individual muscle fibres get bigger (*hypertrophy*). The opposite happens in an endurance horse, where the fibres become smaller. This reduces the distance that oxygen has to travel within the fibres to reach the mitochondria inside them. Human marathon runners are lean and slightly-muscled because their muscles are composed of small muscle fibres. Human sprinters appear muscled because their muscle fibres are much larger. The same difference can be seen between a showjumper and an Arab endurance horse.

Circulatory System

The size of the heart varies with both size and breed. Although larger horses will generally have larger hearts, pound for pound, Thoroughbreds have much larger hearts than heavier breeds such as warmbloods. A 500kg Thoroughbred may have a heart that weighs 5kg and can beat nearly four times a second during a gallop, pumping around one litre of blood with each beat. This equates to enough blood being pumped every minute to fill a normal-sized bath! The heart is composed of cardiac muscle, and this has the capacity to increase through training. If the training is primarily aerobic (below heart rates of roughly 180bpm) the chambers of the heart become larger so that the volume of blood pumped on each beat (known as the stroke volume) increases. The result is that after training at the same heart rate, more blood is pumped out; or, that after training, to pump the same amount of blood around the body each minute, the heart does not have to beat so often (or work so hard). This is why, after training, heart rates are lower during exercise at the same speed. Training also results in an increase in the number of red blood cells and hence the volume in circulation, which allows more oxygen to be delivered to the muscles. The capacity of the muscles to use oxygen is also increased by training. The net result is that the capacity to use oxygen increases with training, and the horse can work faster before having to rely on anaerobic metabolism. Red blood cells have a limited lifespan (between four and five months). As the horse works harder, their lifespan decreases. A blood cell can travel hundreds of miles through blood vessels in the course of its life and, eventually, it wears out. The old, worn-out, damaged, red blood cells are removed by the spleen. The young cells which replace the old have a greater oxygen-carrying capacity.

Respiratory System

The respiratory system of the horse does not respond to training. The amount of air moved in and out of the lungs each minute at a fast canter after training will be the same whether the horse is fit or unfit. This is contrary to what is stated in most equestrian books but it is a fact based on a number of scientific studies which all concluded that the lungs and the airways do not respond to training. This is not surprising, as the lungs and airways contain relatively little muscle.

Bone

Bone responds to the stress of loading (taking weight) during exercise by laying down more bone cells and increasing in mass, which increases strength. If bone is not subjected to stress (for example, during a period of box rest), a proportion of the cells are reabsorbed, reducing the mass and strength. Only very short periods—several minutes—of daily loading are required to maintain bone development or mass. When bone is overloaded it responds by rapidly laying down bone cells to try and adapt. When this occurs on the front of the cannon bone it is referred to as *sore shins*, which is a condition common in young racehorses and is a warning to reduce the intensity and volume (amount) of training.

Tendons

Tendons are made of *collagen* (which, on a weight-for-weight basis, is as strong as steel), *elastin* (which allows the tendon to stretch, absorb and store energy) and a small number of living tendon cells known as *tenocytes*. Tendons link muscle to bone and transmit the forces generated by the locomotory muscles to the bones or joints. Around 95% of a tendon is made up of Type I collagen. Most studies suggest that tendons do not change in size with training. In contrast to bone and muscle, the tendons of a horse older than one year appear to have very limited capacity to respond beneficially to exercise training, and limited capacity for repair. We can think of a tendon being the equivalent of a metal spring. If it is stretched and compressed, the more it is stretched and the greater the force with which it is compressed, and the more times this happens, it will eventually reach a point where it breaks. Whilst some tendon injuries undoubtedly occur due to a slip or a misplaced limb, the majority are almost certainly caused by wear-and-tear or, put simply, over-use.

How to Take a Horse's Respiration Rate

The normal respiration or breathing rate of a horse is around 12 breaths per minute. This can be checked by watching the movement of a horse's flanks, which can be done in or out of the saddle or by watching the nostrils. Each combination of an in-and-out movement is counted as one breath. The number of breaths should be counted for at least thirty seconds, or ideally a whole minute. Respiratory rate may be increased above the normal rate at rest for an hour or more after exercise, after travelling, in hot weather, or in the case of an infection or respiratory disease. The horse should be calm and resting when an assessment of respiratory rate is made.

Good Management to Reduce Injuries

Some injuries and mishaps are just accidents: they may be caused by bad luck, and it would have been very difficult or even impossible to have prevented them. However, there are ways in which you can help to reduce the risk of your horse or pony being injured during training or competition. It is advisable to be familiar with your horse's resting temperature, pulse and respiration rates. Not only can this be helpful to assess response to exercise and training (*see* page 33), any significant deviation from normal could be a sign that something is wrong.

Soundness

Lameness is the most common cause for calling a vet. Try to train on as good a surface as you can for flatwork, jumping and fitness work. Try to avoid very hard or very soft surfaces. Hard surfaces increase the risk of bone and joint injury. Soft surfaces increase the risk of muscle and tendon injury. If you have no choice but to train on very hard or very soft surfaces, reduce the amount of training time. Get into the habit of trotting your horse or pony in hand to check that he is sound. It is better to ask someone else to do this for you. If you are not sure what to look for, then consult your vet (who will be more than happy to tell you).

Cough

After lameness, the next most common cause for calling a vet is respiratory disease. Healthy horses do not cough. If your horse or pony is coughing—even if only a few times a day—then it is an indication for you to call out your vet!

Rectal Temperature Check

Before you tack up your horse or pony or before you put him in a trailer or horsebox to go to a competition, check his rectal temperature. When horses pick up an infection (from a virus or a bacteria) there is a period of a few days when there are no signs of infection. The first sign may be a small increase in body temperature which then returns to normal, followed a day or so later by a bigger rise in temperature. This lasts for longer as the horse starts to show other clinical signs (cough, nasal discharge, going off feed). The first—smaller and shorter—increase in temperature is referred to as a *spike*. The horse or pony is starting to become sick but you cannot yet see the external signs. If you travel, train or compete as your horse is becoming ill, this can make things worse because exercise and travel stress decrease the body's ability to fight infection.

If you adopt the habit of taking regular rectal temperatures, you will get to know your horse or pony's normal values. It is important to try and take the temperature at the same times each day—say, first thing in the morning and at a certain time each evening—as the horse's temperature changes over 24 hours. It will be lowest early in the morning and higher in the evening. If the temperature is more than 0.5°C higher than normal it is not advisable to travel or to exercise your horse or pony.

How to Take a Horse's Pulse Rate

The horse's normal resting pulse rate is usually between 30 and 40 beats per minute (*bpm*). The best way to take the pulse is to place your first and second fingers gently onto the artery at the point where it runs across the inside edge of the left cheekbone. Count the pulse for 15 seconds and then multiply by four—and this will give you the pulse rate. It is also possible to take the horse's pulse rate from the saddle by leaning down and pressing the back of your left hand against the ribs in front of the girth. When horses are excited their heart rate will be higher than normal. The heart rate may also be higher than normal for some time after exercise or travelling. An elevated heart rate can also be associated with pain.

How to Take a Horse's Temperature

The horse has, at rest, a normal rectal temperature of between 37.5 and 38.5°C (99.5 and 101.3°F). The temperature can be taken using a traditional glass or a digital veterinary thermometer, which should be lubricated with petroleum jelly and inserted into the horse's rectum as shown below. The thermometer should be held firmly in place against the side wall of the rectum for at least one minute before being removed and read.

The horse's temperature will be around 0.3 to 0.5°C lower first thing in the morning than in the evening, and you may also find that the reading may be increased for several hours after exercise or after travelling. It is a good idea to get into the routine of taking your horse or pony's temperature first thing in the morning. If it is more than 0.5°C above his normal reading it would be unwise to exercise or travel him and someone should take his temperature more regularly every three to four hours. If your horse or pony's temperature is more than 1°C above his normal reading and if he is showing other clinical signs (such as coughing, wheezing, or nasal discharge) then you should consult your vet.

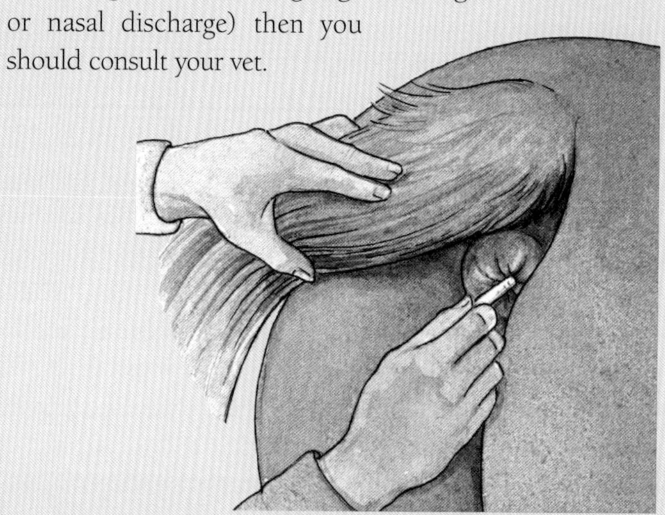

Conclusion

Getting your horse or pony to the appropriate level of fitness is a complex, ongoing process, and you will have the best chance of success if, right from the start, every aspect of your horse's needs and health is checked and found to be in good order.

In addition to regular worming and vaccinations, he should have had a visit from a dental technician to ensure that there are no sharp points on his teeth or any other problems inside the mouth which could affect his acceptance of the bit. Your farrier should confirm that the horse's feet are in good enough condition to begin the fitness programme, and the horse should be shod regularly. The fit of the saddle should be checked—both before you begin work and at six-monthly intervals thereafter—as the profile of the back will change as the horse builds up muscle in this area. A six-monthly check-up from a physiotherapist would also be beneficial, to ensure that the horse's back and general musculature are in good shape.

The feeding plan and day-to-day care that you give your horse is also important. Running your hands carefully over his legs every day to check for heat, lumps and bumps could alert you to a problem in the making; so could taking note of any small difference in his physical condition, his behaviour or his attitude to work.

Building a good relationship with your vet should be an essential part of your plans; consult him or her promptly when problems occur rather than carrying on working in the hope that somehow things will sort themselves out.

The amount of time and trouble you spend on getting your horse fit now will be repaid many times over in the future, so that you will be riding your fit, healthy and happy horse for many years to come.

Index